Country Kitchen
COOKBOOK

by Darlene Kronschnabel

D1312479

Ideals Publishing Corp.

Milwaukee, Wisconsin

CONTENTS

ISBN 0-89542-633-1

COPYRIGHT © MCMLXXV BY IDEALS PUBLISHING CORPORATION
MILWAUKEE, WISCONSIN 53226
ALL RIGHTS RESERVED. PRINTED AND BOUND IN U.S.A.
PUBLISHED SIMULTANEOUSLY IN CANADA

BREADS

Corn bread is as popular in country kitchens as apple pie. And it is a native American dish. Bread made from Indian corn helped the colonists survive the critical winters in their new land.

Corn bread, as popular as ever, goes by many different names. In some areas it is called hoecake, ashcake, johnnycake, or journeycake.

GRANNY'S APPLE CORN BREAD

2 c. yellow cornmeal	2 T. butter, melted
1/4 c. sugar	2 eggs, beaten
1 1/2 t. salt	1 t. soda
2 c. sour milk	1 T. cold water
7/8 c. raw chopped apple	

In the top of a double boiler, mix the cornmeal, sugar, salt, milk and butter. Set over hot water and cook about 10 minutes. Cool, and add eggs, soda dissolved in water, and apples. Bake in greased 8 x 8 x 2-inch pan at 400° about 25 minutes or until done. Makes 8 large squares.

PINEAPPLE CORN BREAD

2 c. flour	1 egg, slightly beaten
5 t. baking powder	1 c. milk
1/4 t. baking soda	3/4 c. crushed pineapple, well-drained
1 1/2 t. salt	
1/2 c. sugar	
1 c. yellow cornmeal	1/4 c. butter, melted

Sift flour, baking powder, soda, salt and sugar; sift again and add cornmeal; mix thoroughly. Combine egg, milk, crushed pineapple and melted butter (slightly cooled); pour into flour mixture and stir just enough to moisten the dry ingredients. Do not beat. Turn into a greased square pan (8 x 8 x 2 inches) and bake in a 350° oven about 50 minutes. Cut into squares and serve hot.

CORNMEAL SPOON BREAD

3/4 c. yellow cornmeal
1 T. sugar
1/2 t. salt
2 c. milk
1/4 c. butter
4 eggs, separated

Preheat oven to 375°. Lightly grease a 1 1/2 quart casserole. Mix cornmeal, sugar and salt in three-quart saucepan. Add milk and butter and heat mixture to boiling point. Stir constantly until thickened. Remove from heat. Beat egg yolks in small bowl. Gradually stir about 1/3 cup of hot cornmeal mixture into yolks, a tablespoon at a time. Stir egg yolk mixture into remaining cornmeal mixture; mix thoroughly. Cool to lukewarm. Beat egg whites in large bowl with clean eggbeater until stiff peaks form; gradually fold in cornmeal mixture. Pour into prepared casserole. Bake 40 minutes. Serve immediately. Makes 6 to 8 servings.

SWEET CORN BREAD

1 c. coarsely ground cornmeal	1 1/2 c. sugar
2 c. white flour	4 large eggs, separated
1 T. baking powder	1 c. rich milk or half-and-half
1/2 t. salt	1 t. vanilla extract
3/4 c. butter, melted	

Combine the cornmeal, flour, baking powder, salt and sugar. Combine the egg yolks, milk, vanilla and melted butter. Stir into the dry ingredients until they are thoroughly moistened. Beat the egg whites until stiff and fold into the batter carefully. Pour into a 3-quart shallow baking pan that has been buttered well. Bake at 350° for 30 minutes, or until it tests done. If desired, 2 8-inch square pans may be used.

Sally Lunn is a delicious old-time bread brought to the American Colonies by early English settlers. Some recipes that have been popular for several hundred years call Sally Lunn a bread, a bun, and even a bread cake.

According to tradition, Sally Lunn originated in Bath, England and was named for a young lady who made it popular. It is said she sold buns on the streets crying, "Solet Lune," to advertise her bread. In time the name became Sally Lunn.

By the time the great English recipe reached America, the popular English buns became a bread baked in a Turk's head mold. Another Americanization of the recipe turned Sally Lunn into a sweet bread cake using cornmeal—delicious with fresh fruits and whipped cream.

CORN STICKS

1 c. flour
1 c. cornmeal
½ t. baking soda
1 t. salt
1 egg, beaten
1 c. sour milk or buttermilk
1 T. butter, melted

Mix and sift flour, cornmeal, soda and salt. Combine egg and milk. Add to flour mixture, stirring until well mixed. Stir in butter. Turn into greased breadstick pans and bake in 425° oven 15 to 20 minutes. Makes 12 corn sticks. To use sweet instead of sour milk, substitute 3 teaspoons baking powder for soda. For corn bread, bake in greased, shallow pan in 400° oven about 30 minutes.

SALLY LUNN
(Baking Powder)

2¼ c. flour
1 t. salt
2 T. sugar
4 t. baking powder
⅓ c. butter
3 eggs, separated
1 c. milk

Sift the dry ingredients three times. Cut the butter into the dry ingredients as for pastry. Beat the egg yolks thoroughly and add the milk. Stir into the dry ingredients. Beat egg whites until stiff and fold into mixture. Pour batter into buttered muffin tins. Bake at 400° for 30 minutes or until done.

CORN SALLY LUNN

1 c. yellow cornmeal
2 c. white flour
1 T. baking powder
1 t. salt
¾ c. butter, melted
1¼ c. sugar
4 eggs, separated
1 c. top milk or half-and-half
1 t. vanilla extract

Sift together the cornmeal, flour, baking powder, sugar and salt. Blend the egg yolks, milk, vanilla and melted butter. Stir this mixture into the dry ingredients until they are well mixed. Beat the egg whites until stiff and fold carefully into the batter. Pour into a well-buttered, shallow, 3-quart pan. Bake at 350° for 30 minutes or until the cake tests done. Serve warm with fresh fruit and whipped cream.

SALLY LUNN
(Yeast)

⅓ c. sugar
½ c. butter
2 t. salt
1 c. rich milk, scalded and cooled
1½ pkgs. active dry yeast
¼ c. lukewarm water
3 medium eggs, beaten
4 c. flour

Cream the butter, sugar and salt. Add the cooled milk. Dissolve the yeast in the water and add to the creamed mixture along with the beaten eggs. Add the flour a little at a time, beating well after each addition. Cover and let rise until doubled. Then punch down and pour into a well-greased bundt, loaf or 10-inch angel food cake pan. Cover and let rise again. Bake in a 350° oven for about 40 minutes or until the bread is golden brown and tests done.

The traditional American breakfast of steaming pancakes with melted butter, dripping with maple syrup is a country kitchen favorite, but did not originate in this country.

Settlers brought the unique but widely popular bread to the New World. These tasty pancakes are known across the country as hot cakes, griddle cakes and flapjacks, and as flannel cakes in logging camps.

Pancakes are popular in most parts of the world where grain is a major crop. No one knows who invented pancakes. They predate leavened bread and no doubt are evidence of early man's mixing of pounded grain and water. The combination was not fried but spread on a flat rock in the hot sun to dry.

Pancakes became so popular that they even have a special day set aside for them. "Shrove Tuesday," the day before the start of Lent, is traditionally a day to serve pancakes. It was the day to use up all the milk, eggs and fat, which were not allowed during the strict days of Lent.

The pancake is still at home at all meals, from country kitchens to elegant dining rooms.

APPLE CORN CAKES

1 egg, slightly beaten	½ t. baking soda
	½ t. salt
2 T. lard, melted	1 T. sugar
1 c. buttermilk	1½ c. apples
1 c. cornmeal	peeled, chopped

Stir together liquid ingredients; blend into sifted dry ingredients. Add chopped apples. Bake on pre-heated lightly greased griddle. Makes about 20 2-inch cakes. Serve with cinnamon applesauce.

NORWEGIAN PANCAKES

4 eggs	¼ t. salt
2 c. milk	Butter
1 c. flour	

Beat eggs at high speed, then lower speed and add milk, flour and salt. Beat until smooth. Mixture should be the consistency of thick cream. Heat 2 or 3 heavy iron skillets (No. 8 is an excellent size) and butter them lightly. Pour ¼ cup batter into each, tilting the pans to cover the entire surface. When bubbles form on top, turn quickly and brown the other side. Fold pancakes in half, then in quarters to serve. Serve with jelly or maple syrup.

TASTY MAPLE SAUCE

2 T. cornstarch
¼ t. salt
2 c. maple blended syrup
4 T. butter

Combine all ingredients in a 1 quart saucepan. Bring to boil over medium heat. Simmer 3 minutes, stirring constantly. Serve hot over buckwheat pancakes. Makes 2 cups.

BUTTERMILK PANCAKES

2 eggs, beaten	2 t. baking powder
2½ c. buttermilk	1 t. salt
2½ c. flour	2 T. sugar
1 t. baking soda	¼ c. butter, melted

Combine well-beaten eggs and buttermilk in large bowl. Sift together flour, baking soda, baking powder, salt and sugar. Stir into egg mixture. Blend until smooth. Add melted butter. Drop by ladle or tablespoon on hot, lightly greased griddle. Brown on both sides until done. Makes 20 to 24 medium-sized pancakes.

DESSERT PANCAKES

¼ c. butter, softened	¼ c. flour
¼ c. sugar	½ c. milk
¼ t. salt	¼ t. vanilla
5 medium eggs, separated	Sugar
	Cinnamon

Cream together the butter, sugar and salt; add the egg yolks and beat well. Stir in the flour and then the milk. Beat the egg whites until stiff but not dry, add the vanilla, and fold into the batter. Grease a cast-iron griddle with unsalted butter and pour less than ¼ cup of batter onto it. Do not tip or spread. These pancakes will be 5 or 6 inches across and about ¼ inch thick while baking. Brown lightly on one side only, lift gently onto a flat ovenproof dish and set in a 250° oven. Sprinkle a little sugar and cinnamon on the uncooked surface of each pancake before placing the next one on top of it. Continue until there are 5 layers, then start another stack. Bake for 15 to 20 minutes or until the top is delicately brown. Cut pie-fashion. Serve at once. Makes 6 servings.

Coffee and fresh doughnuts are old-fashioned country kitchen treats, thanks to early Dutch settlers. They brought the "olykoeks" or oily cakes with them to the New World. But it took an ingenious Yankee mother to spread their fame around the world.

One interesting account claims that by 1803, fried pastries were popular in the New England states. About that time a sea captain's mother made up a dough recipe for deep frying that contained nutmeg, cinnamon and lemon rind.

Her idea was to prepare a pastry using lemon that could be taken to sea to help prevent scurvy and colds. The pastries were intended to be eaten by dunking in hot black coffee or tea.

She inserted hazelnuts in the center of the pastries to be sure the centers cooked all the way through and named her invention doughnuts.

It is said her son's ship sailed with 1500 doughnuts. By the time he returned home, doughnuts were popular in all ports of call. The doughnuts' popularity then spread across America.

POTATO DOUGHNUTS

- 1 c. sieved cooked potatoes (warm or cold)
- 1 c. liquid (reserved from cooking potatoes)
- ¾ c. vegetable shortening
- ½ c. sugar
- 1 T. salt
- 1 pkg. active dry yeast
- ¾ c. warm water (105° to 115°)
- 2 eggs, beaten
- 5 to 6 c. flour
  Shortening

Mix potatoes, potato liquid, shortening, sugar and salt. Dissolve yeast in warm water; stir into potato mixture. Stir in eggs and enough flour to make dough easy to handle. Turn dough onto lightly floured surface; knead until smooth and elastic, 5 to 8 minutes. Place in greased bowl; turn greased side up. (Don't punch down.) Cover; let rise until double, 1 to 1½ hours. Pat out dough on lightly-floured surface to ¾-inch thickness. Cut doughnuts with floured 2½-inch cutter. Let rise until double, about 1 hour. Heat 3 to 4 inches of shortening to 375° in heavy pan. Fry doughnuts 2 to 3 minutes on each side, or until golden. Drain on paper toweling. If desired, glaze or roll in sugar. Makes about 3 dozen.

OLD-FASHIONED DOUGHNUTS

- 2¼ c. flour
- ½ t. salt
- 3 t. baking powder
- ½ t. ground cinnamon
- ¼ t. ground nutmeg
- ½ c. sugar
- 1 egg
- ½ c. milk
- 1 t. grated lemon rind
- 2 T. butter, melted
  Shortening or pure vegetable oil
  Confectioners' sugar

Sift together flour, salt, baking powder, spices and sugar. Beat egg; stir in milk, lemon rind and melted butter. Blend into flour mixture, stirring until all flour is moistened. Chill 15 minutes. Roll dough out to ½-inch thickness on well-floured board. Cut with 3-inch floured doughnut cutter, dipping cutter into flour each time it is used. Heat shortening (it should be 1½ to 2 inches deep) in a heavy saucepan or electric skillet to 375° on deep-frying thermometer. Drop doughnuts gently into fat, 3 or 4 at a time. As they rise to surface, turn with fork or slotted spoon to brown other side. It will take about 3 minutes. Lift doughnuts from fat with slotted spoon. Drain well on paper towels. Serve plain or dusted with confectioners' sugar. Makes about 1 dozen.

HOLY POKES

Form bread dough, which has risen once, into balls the size of large marbles. Let rise again until it has doubled in volume. Slip dough balls into a kettle of fat that has been heated to 360° and fry until golden brown. Drain and serve with plenty of butter.

PEACHY PLUM FRITTERS

1½ c. flour
¼ c. sugar
2 t. baking powder
½ t. salt
½ to ¾ c. milk
1 egg, beaten
1 t. vanilla extract
1 c. chopped fresh peaches
½ c. chopped fresh plums
¼ c. chopped nuts
    Lard for deep frying
    Granulated or confectioners' sugar
    (optional)

Stir together dry ingredients. Combine ½ cup milk, egg, vanilla, fruits and nuts; add all at once to flour mixture, stirring until well blended. If necessary, stir in more milk to make a medium-thick batter. Drop by rounded tablespoonfuls into 2 to 3 inches of preheated 375° lard. Fry until golden brown, 3 to 4 minutes, turning once. Drain on absorbent paper. Serve warm coated with granulated or confectioners' sugar, if desired. Makes 18 fritters.

HONEY DOUGHNUTS

1 pkg. active dry yeast
¼ c. warm water (110° - 115°)
9 c. sifted flour
3 c. milk, scalded and cooled to lukewarm
½ c. butter
4 T. honey
2 eggs, beaten
1½ t. salt

Soften yeast in warm water. Let stand 5 to 10 minutes. Add 4 cups flour gradually to the milk, beating until smooth. Stir in the yeast. Cover; let rise in a warm place until doubled. Cream the butter until softened. Blend in the honey. Add the eggs, one at a time, beating well after each addition. Beat this mixture gradually into yeast mixture. Stir in salt and remaining flour. Cover; let rise until doubled. Punch down dough; divide into four portions. On a floured surface, roll out each portion about ½-inch thick. Cut with floured doughnut cutter. Cover; let rise until doubled. Fry in deep fat heated to 370° 3 to 4 minutes, turning doughnuts to brown evenly. Remove from fat; drain on absorbent paper. Makes about 3½ dozen doughnuts.

RAISED DOUGHNUTS

1 c. milk
1 pkg. active dry yeast
¼ c. lukewarm water
1 c. brown sugar, firmly packed
6 c. flour
1 t. salt
1 t. cinnamon or nutmeg
2 eggs, beaten
1 c. softened butter
    Fat for deep frying

Scald milk, then cool to lukewarm. Sprinkle yeast over lukewarm water to dissolve. Sift together sugar, flour, salt and cinnamon or nutmeg. Combine milk and yeast in a large bowl. Work in the flour with your hands (dough will be very heavy). Then stir in beaten eggs. Cover and let rise in a warm place until double in size. Punch down the dough, then work in the butter with your hands until dough is smooth and well blended. Roll about ½-inch thick on a lightly floured board and cut with a doughnut cutter. Place doughnuts on a tray lined with wax paper, cover again and let rise in a warm place until light and puffy. Drop several at a time into deep fat preheated to 375° on a deep fat thermometer or until a 1-inch cube of bread browns in 60 seconds. Fry until nicely browned on both sides. Lift from fat, drain on paper towels, and sprinkle with confectioners' sugar, granulated sugar or a mixture of sugar and cinnamon. Makes about 40.

ORANGE GLAZE

Add 1 teaspoon grated orange peel and 3 tablespoons orange juice or apple cider to 2 cups sifted confectioners' sugar. Glaze doughnuts while they are still warm.

MAPLE GLAZE

Combine 1 pound sifted confectioners' sugar with 6 tablespoons boiling water and ½ teaspoon maple extract to make a thin, smooth glaze. Add a few drops more water if glaze is too thick to coat doughnuts lightly.

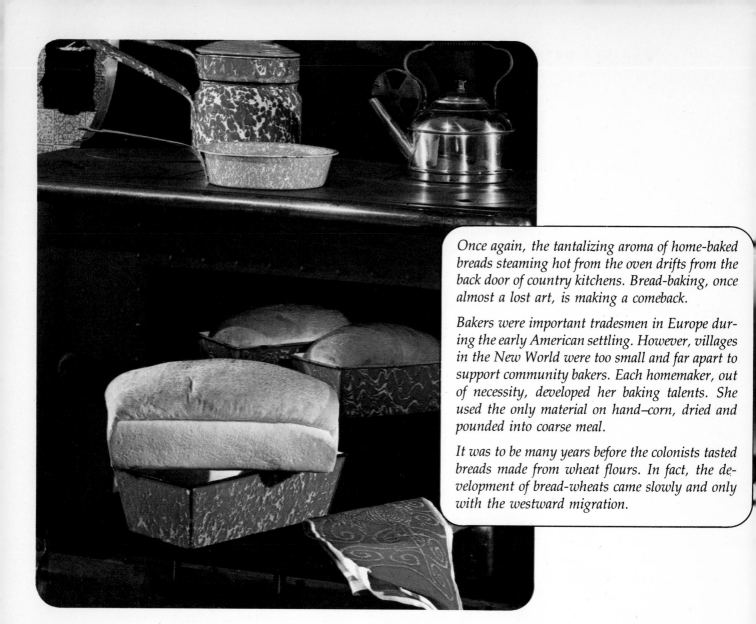

Once again, the tantalizing aroma of home-baked breads steaming hot from the oven drifts from the back door of country kitchens. Bread-baking, once almost a lost art, is making a comeback.

Bakers were important tradesmen in Europe during the early American settling. However, villages in the New World were too small and far apart to support community bakers. Each homemaker, out of necessity, developed her baking talents. She used the only material on hand—corn, dried and pounded into coarse meal.

It was to be many years before the colonists tasted breads made from wheat flours. In fact, the development of bread-wheats came slowly and only with the westward migration.

WHITE BREAD

2 c. milk, scalded and cooled to lukewarm
2 c. lukewarm water
2 T. salt
5 T. sugar
5 T. butter, melted and slightly cooled
2 cakes compressed yeast
12 to 12½ c. flour

Put lukewarm liquids into mixing bowl. Crumble yeast into liquids and stir until dissolved. Measure salt and sugar and stir into yeast solution. Let stand 5 minutes. Add butter and stir well. Sift and measure flour. Add 6 cups of flour and beat until smooth. Add most of remaining flour. Stir to mix thoroughly. Turn out onto lightly floured board. Knead lightly, but thoroughly for 10 minutes. Round up dough and place in a large greased bowl and turn once to bring greased side up. Cover with cloth and set in a warm place until double in size. Knead down and let rise until almost double in size. Cut dough into 4 equal portions. Shape into loaves and place in well-greased bread pans. Cover lightly and set in warm place. Allow to rise until sides of dough have reached top of pan and corners are filled. Bake in 400° oven for 10 minutes. Reduce heat to 350° and bake 25 to 30 minutes or until bread is golden brown and sounds hollow when tapped. Turn out of pans and allow to cool before storing. Makes 4 loaves.

CINNAMON BREAD

2 pkgs. active dry yeast
½ c. warm water
1 c. milk, scalded
½ c. butter
⅓ c. honey
1 t. salt
1 egg, slightly beaten
5 to 5½ c. flour
¾ c. wheat germ

Dissolve yeast in warm water. Let stand. Pour scalded milk over butter. Stir to melt butter. Add honey and salt. Add beaten egg. Mix well. Combine yeast, milk and egg mixtures. Blend well. Add 2½ cups flour and beat until smooth. Add the wheat germ and beat until smooth again. Add additional flour to make a soft dough. Knead gently for a few minutes to make a smooth but soft dough. Cover and let rise until double. Divide in half; roll each half to 7 x 12-inch rectangle. Brush with slightly beaten egg white and sprinkle with mixture of ½ cup sugar, 1 tablespoon cinnamon and ½ cup finely chopped nuts. Roll like jelly roll, put in greased loaf pan 9 x 5 x 3. Bake 35-40 minutes at 375°.

RYE BREAD

1 c. milk
2 T. honey
1 T. sugar
1 T. salt
1 T. butter
¾ c. warm water
1 pkg. active dry yeast
1 T. caraway seeds
2½ c. unsifted rye flour
2½ c. unsifted white flour (about)
¼ c. cornmeal
1 egg white
2 T. water

Scald milk; add honey, sugar, salt and butter. Cool to lukewarm. Measure warm water into large warm bowl. Sprinkle in yeast; stir until dissolved. Add lukewarm milk mixture. Add caraway seeds and rye flour; beat well. Add enough white flour to make a soft dough. Turn dough out onto lightly floured board; knead until smooth and elastic, about 7 minutes. Place in greased bowl, turning to grease top. Cover; let rise in warm place, until doubled in bulk, about 1½ hours. Turn out onto lightly floured board. Divide dough in half; form each piece into a smooth ball. Flatten each piece slightly. Roll lightly on board to form loaves. Sprinkle two greased baking sheets with cornmeal. Place breads on baking sheets. Combine egg white and water; brush breads. Let rise, uncovered, in warm place, for 35 minutes. Bake in 400° oven 25 minutes. Cool on wire racks. Makes 2 loaves.

BUCKWHEAT BREAD

1 pkg. active dry yeast
1 T. brown sugar
¼ c. lukewarm water
1 c. milk
¼ c. water
1 T. salt
3 T. brown sugar
3 T. butter
2 c. whole wheat flour
1½ c. buckwheat flour

Dissolve the yeast with 1 tablespoon of sugar in lukewarm water until frothy. Scald the milk and water and add the salt, remaining sugar and butter. Mix the flours in a large mixing bowl. When the milk mixture is lukewarm mix it with the yeast and add to the flour. Beat very hard for 3 minutes with a rubber spatula. A little more warm water or flour may be needed to make a spongy dough that is not too soft. Put the bowl in a dishpan of hot water, cover with a towel and let the dough rise an hour or more until it is light. Beat again 2 or 3 minutes; put the dough in a greased bread pan. Set it in warm water again to rise an hour. Put the pan in a cold oven. Set at 400° and bake 15 minutes; turn heat to 350° and continue baking about 35 minutes more. Makes 1 loaf.

POTATO BREAD

2 c. milk, scalded
3 c. potato water
2 cakes compressed yeast
2 T. butter
4 t. salt
2 T. sugar
12 to 12½ c. flour

Scald milk, stir in butter, salt and sugar. Add potato water. Cool to lukewarm. Crumble in yeast. Stir until dissolved. Add 4 cups flour; beat until smooth. Add enough additional flour to make a soft dough. Turn out onto lightly floured board. Knead until smooth and elastic, about 8-10 minutes. Form into smooth ball. Place in greased bowl, turning to grease top. Cover; let rise in warm place until doubled in bulk, about 1 hour. Punch down. Divide dough in quarters. Shape each into a loaf. Place each loaf in a greased 9 x 5 x 3-inch bread pan. Cover; let rise in warm place, free from draft, until doubled in bulk, about 1 hour. Bake in 400° oven about 30 minutes. Remove from pans and cool.

BROWN BREAD

1½ c. all-purpose flour	½ c. seedless raisins
1½ c. rye flour	½ c. walnuts
1 c. yellow cornmeal	2 c. buttermilk
1 t. baking soda	½ c. dark molasses
1 t. salt	Butter

Mix together flour, rye flour, cornmeal, baking soda and salt. Add raisins and nuts. Slowly add buttermilk and molasses alternately to dry ingredients; beat after each addition. Pour batter into greased 9 x 5 x 3-inch loaf pan. Bake at 375° for 50 minutes or until done. Remove from oven and let stand in pan 5 minutes. Loosen sides with knife and turn out on wire rack. Brush with butter while still warm. Makes 1 loaf.

STEAMED BROWN BREAD

1 c. white flour
1 c. whole wheat flour
1 c. cornmeal
1½ t. salt
½ c. sugar
1 t. baking soda
½ c. molasses
1½ c. buttermilk
2 T. melted shortening

Sift flour, whole wheat flour, cornmeal, salt and sugar together. Mix soda and molasses. Add buttermilk and molasses to the dry mixture. Add shortening. Mix well. Fill a greased 2½-quart pudding mold ¾ full and steam 3 hours. Remove cover from pan and allow to cool 20 minutes. Remove to wire rack and finish cooling.

APPLESAUCE BROWN BREAD

2 c. whole wheat flour
1 c. cornmeal
¾ t. salt
1 t. baking soda
1 c. buttermilk
1 c. dark molasses
¾ c. sweetened applesauce
¾ c. raisins

Combine dry ingredients in large mixing bowl. Add buttermilk and molasses and beat until smooth. Mixture will be thick. Fold in applesauce and raisins. Turn into greased 9-inch square baking pan and bake in 350° oven 35 minutes or until done. Cool 10 minutes in pan, then remove from pan and cool on wire rack. Cut into squares. Makes 16 squares.

APRICOT BRAN BREAD

1 c. finely cut, dried apricots	⅓ c. vegetable oil
¾ c. sugar	1½ c. flour
1½ c. cereal bran	3 t. baking powder
1 c. milk	1 t. salt
2 eggs, slightly beaten	1 T. sugar

Pour enough boiling water over apricots to cover; let stand 10 minutes. Drain well; combine apricots and ¾ cup sugar. Set aside. Measure cereal bran and milk into large mixing bowl; stir until combined. Let stand 1-2 minutes or until most of the liquid is absorbed. Add eggs and oil to cereal mixture; beat well. Sift together flour, baking powder and salt. Add sifted dry ingredients to cereal mixture; stir only until combined. Gently fold in apricot mixture. Spread batter evenly in well-greased, waxed paper-lined 9 x 5 x 3-inch loaf pan. Sprinkle top with the one tablespoon sugar. Bake at 350° for about one hour or until toothpick inserted near center comes out clean. Let stand until thoroughly cooled before slicing. Makes one loaf.

BLUEBERRY BUCKLE

½ c. sugar	2 t. baking
¼ c. butter,	powder
softened	½ t. salt
1 egg	2½ c. fresh
½ c. milk	blueberries
2 c. flour	

Mix together sugar, butter and egg. Stir in milk. Sift together flour, baking powder and salt. Stir into batter. Mix well. Carefully blend in blueberries. Spread batter into greased and floured 9-inch square pan.

In separate bowl, blend together ½ cup sugar, ⅓ cup flour, ½ teaspoon cinnamon and ¼ cup soft butter. Sprinkle over top of batter. Bake 45 to 50 minutes or until wooden pick inserted in center comes out clean. Serve warm, plain or with ice cream.

CINNAMON COFFEE CAKE

3 c. flour	1 t. salt
1 c. brown sugar,	1 t. vanilla
firmly packed	1 t. baking soda
1 c. granulated sugar	2 eggs
1 T. cinnamon	1 c. buttermilk
1 c. butter	

In large bowl, cut butter into flour, sugars and cinnamon as for pie crust. Reserve ¾ cup of this mixture to use as a topping. To the remaining mixture add the salt, baking soda, vanilla and eggs. Stir until mixed. Add the buttermilk and blend the ingredients until smooth. Do not overbeat. Pour the mixture into a greased and floured angel food pan (spring form). Sprinkle the reserved topping lightly over the top. Bake in 350° oven for 45 minutes or until cake tests done. Cool before removing from the pan. Makes one large coffee cake.

ORANGE COFFEE CAKE

¼ c. butter	2 t. grated
½ c. sugar	orange peel
1 egg	½ c. rolled oats
1¼ c. flour	¼ c. brown sugar
1 t. baking	½ t. cinnamon
powder	2 T. melted butter
1 t. salt	½ c. chopped
½ t. soda	walnuts
½ c. orange juice	½ c. raisins

Cream butter and sugar till light and fluffy. Add egg; beat well. Sift together dry ingredients and add to creamed mixture alternately with orange juice. Stir in orange peel. Turn into greased 8 x 8 x 2-inch baking pan. Combine remaining ingredients and sprinkle over top of batter. Bake in 375° oven 25 minutes or till done.

CARROT COFFEE CAKE

1½ c. flour
2 t. baking powder
½ t. salt
1 t. cinnamon
⅔ c. butter
1 c. sugar
2 large eggs
1 c. raw carrots, pared and coarsely grated, packed firmly (2 very large)
½ c. raisins, rinsed in hot water and drained
½ c. walnuts, chopped (medium fine)

On wax paper sift together the flour, baking powder, salt and cinnamon. Cream butter and sugar; thoroughly beat in eggs, one at a time. Gradually stir in sifted ingredients; add carrots, raisins and walnuts and stir to distribute evenly.

Turn into a 9 x 5 x 3-inch loaf pan (bottom greased, then lined with buttered wax paper). Bake in a 350° oven for 1 hour or until cake tester inserted in center comes out clean. Turn out on wire rack; turn right side up; cool completely. Wrap tightly in plastic wrap and refrigerate overnight. Slice after chilling; wrap slices (piled one on top of the other) and reheat briefly in moderate or hot oven. Serve at once.

Among the many holiday breads popular in country kitchens are hot cross buns.

The cross on hot cross buns dates back to pre-Christian cultures when breads imprinted with various symbols were offered to different gods as sacrifices. The design represented both sun and fire. The sun symbol was a circle divided into quarters by a cross. The four sections represented the seasons.

In England the hot cross bun is associated with the traditions of Good Friday, and until recently was available only on that day. In America, hot cross buns are available throughout the Lenten season.

HOT CROSS BUNS

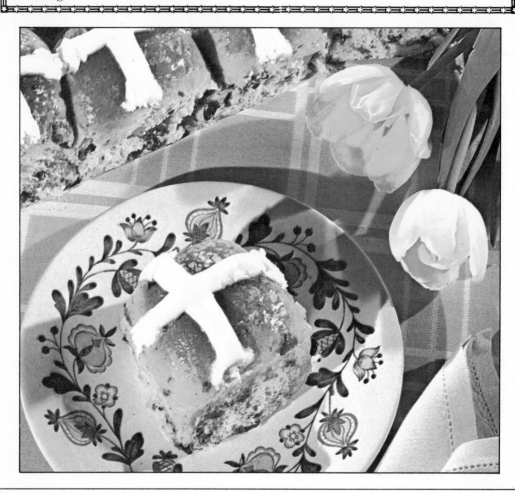

2 c. milk, scalded	8 c. flour
1 c. butter	½ t. salt
1 c. sugar	1½ c. raisins
2 cakes yeast	½ c. candied
dissolved in ⅓ c.	fruit peels
lukewarm water	½ t. cinnamon
2 eggs	or nutmeg

Pour the scalded milk over the butter and sugar and stir to dissolve. Let cool to lukewarm. Add the yeast mixture and eggs and mix well. Gradually add the flour and salt, reserving a small amount of flour to dust the fruits. Add the spice and floured fruits to the dough and knead in thoroughly. Place in a buttered bowl, cover and let rise until doubled. Punch the dough down and turn it out onto a floured board. Shape dough into 30 buns and place on buttered cookie sheets.

Cover and let rise for 30 minutes, then very carefully press the shape of a cross into each bun, using a spatula or the back of a knife. Bake in a 375° oven for 10 minutes, then reduce heat to 350° and continue baking until buns are browned and done, about 10 to 15 minutes longer. Frost either the entire bun or just the shape of the cross.

WHITE FROSTING

Beat one egg white until stiff, adding powdered sugar gradually until mixture is thick. Flavor with one teaspoon lemon juice or vanilla extract, or ¼ teaspoon almond extract. If the frosting thins, add more powdered sugar.

14

CHRISTMAS STOLLEN

1 pkg. active dry yeast	2¼ to 2½ c. flour
¼ c. very warm water (110 to 115°)	½ c. walnuts
¼ c. lukewarm milk, scalded and cooled	¼ c. citron chopped
¼ c. sugar	¼ c. candied cherries, chopped
½ t. salt	1 c. raisins
1 egg	1 T. grated lemon rind
¼ c. butter, softened	

In mixing bowl, dissolve yeast in very warm water. Stir in milk, sugar, salt, soft butter and egg. Combine ½ of the flour with nuts, citron, candied cherries, raisins and lemon rind and add to yeast mixture. Mix with spoon until smooth. Add enough remaining flour to handle easily; mix with hand or spoon. Turn onto lightly floured board; knead until smooth and elastic (about 5 minutes). Place in greased bowl, bring greased side up. Cover and let rise in warm place until double. Punch down and let rise again until almost double, about 30 minutes. Turn onto lightly floured board after dough rises a second time. Spread with soft butter. Fold in half lengthwise. Form into a crescent. Press folded edge firmly so it won't spring open. Place on greased baking sheet. Brush top with butter. Let rise until double, 35 to 45 minutes. Bake in 375° oven for 30 to 35 minutes, or until golden brown. Frost while warm with quick white icing. Decorate with nut halves, pieces of citron and halves of candied cherries to simulate poinsettias. Makes 1 stollen.

QUICK WHITE FROSTING

Sift 1 cup confectioners' sugar. Moisten with 1½ tablespoons cream to spread. Add ½ teaspoon vanilla.

CHRISTMAS LOAF

1 pkg. active dry yeast	4 to 4½ c. flour
½ c. warm water	1 beaten egg
1 c. milk, scalded	1 c. rolled oats
⅓ c. butter	1 c. candied mixed fruit
¼ c. sugar	½ c. chopped nuts
2 t. salt	

Soften yeast in water. Combine milk, butter, sugar and salt; cool to lukewarm. Beat in 1½ cups flour. Add egg and softened yeast; stir in oats, fruit, and nuts. Stir in enough additional flour to make soft dough. Turn out on lightly floured surface and knead till satiny, about 10 minutes. Place dough in greased bowl, turning once to grease surface. Cover and let rise in warm place till doubled, about 1¾ hours. Punch down; cover and let rest 10 minutes. Shape dough into 2 round loaves; place on greased baking sheets. Cover and let rise till doubled, about 1 hour. Bake in 375° oven 30 minutes. Cool and frost with confectioners' sugar frosting. Decorate with candied fruits and nuts. Makes 2 round loaves.

CRANBERRY NUT BREAD

1 c. fresh cranberries	1 t. salt
1 c. sugar	¼ c. shortening
2 c. flour	¾ c. orange juice
1½ t. baking powder	1 t. grated orange rind
½ t. soda	1 egg, well beaten
	½ c. chopped nuts

Sift together flour, sugar, baking powder, soda and salt. Cut in shortening until mixture resembles coarse cornmeal. Combine orange juice and grated rind with well-beaten egg. Pour into dry ingredients and mix just enough to dampen. Fold in chopped nuts and coarsely chopped cranberries. Spoon into greased loaf pan, 9 x 5 x 3. Spread corners and sides a little higher than center. Bake in 350° oven about one hour or until crust is golden brown and toothpick inserted comes out clean. Remove from pan and cool. Store overnight for easy slicing. Makes one loaf.

SOUPS

HAM AND PEA SOUP WITH DUMPLINGS

1 1-lb. pkg. dried split peas
2 qts. boiling water
1 hambone or 2-3 ham hocks
1 c. diced onions
1 c. thinly-sliced celery
½ c. thinly-sliced carrots
   Salt and pepper to taste
   Dumplings

Rinse peas; drain and add to water with hambone or hocks, onion, celery and carrots. Cover and simmer gently for 2 hours. Stir occasionally. About 30 minutes before serving, remove hambone or hocks. Cut off meat and add to soup. Season to taste. Drop dumplings into soup 15 minutes before serving.

Sift together 2 cups flour, 3 teaspoons baking powder and 1 teaspoon salt. Cut in 3 tablespoons shortening. Add 1 cup milk and 1 beaten egg. Mix lightly. Drop from tablespoon into boiling soup to make 8 dumplings. Dip spoon in hot soup before spooning each dumpling so batter will not stick. Cover and cook 15 minutes. Makes 8 servings.

CHICKEN BOOYAH

1 stewing chicken
2 qts. water
1 T. salt
1½ c. potatoes, diced
1½ c. carrots, diced
1 c. celery, diced
1 medium onion, diced
2 c. tomato juice
2 c. canned peas

Cook one stewing chicken in 2 quarts water and 1 tablespoon salt until meat is very tender and can be easily removed from the bones. While chicken is cooking, prepare the diced vegetables. When chicken is tender, remove from broth and add diced vegetables (not peas). Cook until tender. Remove chicken meat from bones and cut into small pieces. When vegetables are tender, add the diced chicken, the tomato juice and the peas. Heat and season to taste. Makes 8 generous servings.

OLD-FASHIONED VEGETABLE SOUP

4 lbs. beef soupbones with generous
   amount of meat
4 qts. water
4 c. tomato juice or stewed tomatoes
1 c. celery stalks and leaves, diced
1 c. chopped onion
¼ c. chopped parsley
2 c. raw carrots, sliced
1 c. diced rutabaga
1 c. diced potatoes
2 c. green peas
2 c. green beans
2 c. shredded cabbage
   Salt and pepper to taste

Place meat and water in a large soup kettle. Bring to boil. Skim surface occasionally. When broth is clear, add tomatoes or juice, celery, onions and parsley. Cover and simmer gently for 2½ hours. Add carrots, rutabaga and potatoes. Simmer ½ hour. Remove soupbone from kettle and cut meat from the bone. Return all to kettle. Add peas, green beans and cabbage. Season to taste. Simmer another ½ hour or until all vegetables are tender. Makes 8 to 10 servings.

OXTAIL SOUP

1 lg. oxtail	1 bay leaf
Flour	6 peppercorns
3 T. fat	3 whole cloves
1 lg. onion, sliced	Salt
2 stalks celery with	4 pts. water
leaves, chopped	1½ T. cornstarch
2 carrots, sliced	

Have the oxtail cut into joints. Wash well and dry, then roll in flour and brown in the hot fat in a large saucepan. When browned evenly, add onions, celery and carrots and brown in the fat for a few minutes. Add water, bay leaf and seasonings, cover and bring slowly to boil, then simmer gently for 3 to 3½ hours, or until meat is tender. Strain the soup and cool quickly until fat sets on top, then skim. Heat soup and add cornstarch, then simmer for 20 minutes or until cornstarch is cooked. Addition of a tablespoon of claret or sherry is good with this soup.

SWEDISH MEATBALLS

4 T. butter	½ t. allspice
⅓ c. minced onion	¼ t. nutmeg
1 egg	1 lb. chuck, ground
½ c. milk	3 T. flour
½ c. fresh bread crumbs	⅛ t. pepper
2½ t. salt	1 c. water
3 t. sugar	¾ c. light cream

Sauté onion until golden brown in 2 tablespoons hot butter in large skillet. Meanwhile, in large mixing bowl, beat egg; add milk and crumbs. Let stand 5 minutes. Add 1¼ teaspoons salt, 2 teaspoons sugar, allspice, nutmeg, meat and onion. Blend well with fork. In same skillet, heat 2 tablespoons butter. Using 2 teaspoons, shape meat mixture into small balls, about ½- to ¾-inch in diameter. Drop some balls into skillet; brown well on all sides; remove to warm casserole. Repeat until all meatballs are browned.

Into the fat left in skillet, stir flour, 1 teaspoon sugar, 1¼ teaspoons salt and pepper; slowly add water and cream; stir until thickened. If desired, return meatballs to gravy and heat well; or serve meatballs in covered casserole; pass gravy. Makes 6 servings.

CORN-CRISPED CHICKEN

- 1 broiler-fryer chicken, cut in serving pieces
- 1 c. cornflake crumbs
- 1 t. salt
- ⅛ t. pepper
- ½ c. evaporated milk

Mix cornflake crumbs with salt and pepper. Line shallow baking pan with aluminum foil. Dip chicken pieces in evaporated milk, then roll immediately in seasoned cornflake crumbs. Place chicken pieces, skin side up, in foil-lined pan; do not crowd. Bake in 350° oven for one hour or until tender. No need to cover or turn chicken while cooking. Makes 4 servings.

PARMESAN FRIED CHICKEN

- 2 broiler-fryer chickens (2½ lbs. each), cut into pieces
- 1 c. flour
- 2 t. salt
- ¼ t. pepper
- 2 t. paprika
- 2 eggs, slightly beaten
- 3 T. milk
- 1⅜ c. grated parmesan cheese
- ⅝ c. dry bread crumbs
- 2 T. butter
- 2 T. shortening
- ¼ c. butter, melted

Heat oven to 400°. Do not use chicken wings (refrigerate or freeze for another meal); remove skin from remaining pieces. Coat chicken with a mixture of flour, salt, pepper and paprika. Combine eggs and milk; dip chicken into egg mixture. Roll in mixture of cheese and bread crumbs. In oven melt the 2 tablespoons of butter and the shortening in jelly roll pan, 15½ x 10½ x 1-inch. Place chicken bone side down in pan. Drizzle with the ¼ cup melted butter. Bake one hour. Cool; cover and chill. Makes six servings.

CHICKEN PAPRIKA CASSEROLE

- 8 oz. egg noodles
- 1 small onion, chopped
- ¼ c. butter
- 2 chickens, about 2 lbs. each, quartered
- ¼ c. flour
- 1 t. salt
- ½ t. pepper
- 1 T. sweet paprika
- 2 c. chicken broth
- 2 T. tomato sauce
- 2 t. Worcestershire sauce
- 2 c. sour cream

Cook noodles until barely tender, drain and put in 5-quart casserole. Sauté onion in the butter. Remove onion and, in same skillet, sauté chicken a few pieces at a time until lightly browned on both sides. Add more butter if necessary. Arrange chicken on noodles. Blend flour into drippings in skillet. Add salt, pepper and paprika. Cook, stirring, 1 or 2 minutes. Add chicken broth and cook until slightly reduced and thickened. Remove from heat, add tomato sauce, Worcestershire sauce and sour cream and pour over chicken. Bake in 350° oven about 1½ hours. Makes 6 to 8 servings.

CREAMED TURKEY

1 T. butter
3 T. minced onion
1 T. chopped parsley
2 c. leftover turkey, diced
2 c. frozen peas
2 T. leftover turkey gravy
 Pinch nutmeg
 Salt and pepper to taste

Melt butter in a skillet and lightly sauté onion and parsley. Stir in turkey, peas, gravy, nutmeg, salt and pepper. Keep warm while preparing the following cream sauce.

Add turkey mixture to cream sauce and blend well. Serve at once over hot, fluffy rice, buttered noodles or hot corn bread, split and generously buttered. Serves 5 to 6.

CREAM SAUCE

1½ T. butter
1½ T. flour
1½ c. top milk or ¾ c. each milk and cream
 2 eggs, beaten

Combine butter, flour and milk in saucepan. Cook, stirring constantly, until smooth and thickened. Season to taste. Quickly stir in eggs.

MUSHROOM & WILD RICE STUFFING

½ c. butter
 1 lb. fresh mushrooms, sliced
½ c. onions, chopped
½ c. parsley, minced
 1 c. celery, chopped
⅔ c. water
 4 c. cooked wild rice
1½ t. salt
⅛ t. pepper

Melt butter in heavy skillet. Add mushrooms and cook over low heat for 5 minutes. Remove mushrooms. Add onion, parsley, and celery to skillet. Cook until onions turn yellow. Add ⅓ cup water along with wild rice and seasonings. Mix well. Add remaining water and the cooked mushrooms. Mix well. Simmer for 15 minutes. Makes 8 servings.

CHICKEN AND DUMPLINGS

1 4- to 5-lb. stewing hen, cut up
3 to 4 sprigs parsley
4 celery stalks with leaves, chopped
1 carrot, diced
½ c. chopped onion
2 t. salt
¼ t. pepper
 Cold water

DUMPLINGS

1½ c. flour
 3 t. baking powder
 ½ t. salt
 ¾ c. milk
 1 t. minced parsley

Fit pieces of prepared chicken into large, heavy kettle. Add vegetables and seasonings. Barely cover with cold water. Cover and heat to boiling. Remove any scum. Reduce heat to simmering and cook until tender —2½ to 3 hours. Fifteen minutes before chicken is done (make sure there is enough water to barely cover chicken), add dumplings prepared as follows:

Combine flour, baking powder and salt. Add milk and stir just until dry ingredients are moistened. Add parsley and stir in. Dip a teaspoon into hot chicken broth, then into dumpling batter; drop a spoonful of batter into chicken broth. Drop all dumplings in quickly. Replace cover and boil gently for 12 minutes. Remove dumplings to platter and arrange pieces of chicken around them. Makes 6 to 8 servings.

APPLE & PRUNE STUFFING

¼ c. butter
 2 qts. tart firm apples, diced
¼ c. brown sugar
¾ t. cinnamon
 1 T. grated lemon rind
 2 c. dry bread cubes
 1 lb. prunes, stewed and pitted

Heat butter in a large heavy skillet; add diced apples, brown sugar, cinnamon and lemon rind. Stir over low heat until apples are just tender but not mushy. Add bread cubes and prunes, tossing together lightly. Makes enough for a 10- to 12-pound goose.

CORNISH PASTIES

2 medium potatoes
1 small onion, finely chopped
½ lb. lean thick pork steak
2 medium carrots
½ lb. lean thick round steak
Salt and pepper to taste

For two good-sized pasties, make enough regular pie crust for a two-crust pie. Divide in half. Roll dough in circle, place ingredients near front edge of crust, dot with butter, and fold other half of crust over ingredients. Pinch together firmly. Pierce with fork to let out excess steam. Bake at 450° for 45 minutes or until tested with toothpick for doneness.

DUTCH "POCKETBOOKS"

Pastry for two double-crust pies
½ lb. finely diced beef chuck
(other meat, such as pork, lamb or liver may be substituted)
2 small potatoes, pared and thinly sliced
2 T. chopped onion
2 small carrots, thinly sliced
2 small turnips, thinly sliced
Salt and pepper to taste
Butter

Prepare pastry and divide into two portions. Roll each portion into a round about 9 inches in diameter and about ¼-inch thick. Using one-half of the meat and vegetables for each pasty and lightly sprinkling each layer with salt and pepper, put a layer of meat and vegetables onto one half of each round. Dot with butter. Fold pastry over filling to form a "pocketbook" and seal edges with the tines of a fork. Slit top of pastry to allow steam to escape while baking. Place pasties on a baking sheet. Bake at 450° for 15 minutes. Reduce heat to 350° and bake 40 minutes longer, or until golden brown. Makes 2 large pasties.

PORK STEAKS

4 pork blade steaks,
½ to ¾ inch thick
2 T. lard
1½ t. salt
¼ t. pepper
4 slices onion, ¼-inch thick
4 slices tomato, ½-inch thick
4 green pepper rings,
¼-inch thick

Brown steaks in lard. Remove steaks from pan and arrange in shallow casserole or baking pan. Season with salt and pepper. Cover and bake in a 350° oven for 30 minutes. Remove from oven and place a slice of onion, a slice of tomato and a slice of green pepper on each steak. Cover and return to oven for another 15 minutes.

SAUSAGE PASTIES

Pastry for double-crust pie
½ lb. bulk pork sausage
¼ c. onion, finely chopped
2½ c. mashed turnips
1 c. mashed potatoes
1 t. salt
⅛ t. pepper

In a large skillet, brown sausage, crumbling meat with a fork as it cooks. Remove with a slotted spoon and place in a large bowl; set aside. Add onion to skillet and sauté until transparent, about 5 minutes. Remove with a slotted spoon and add to sausage. Add turnips, potatoes, salt and pepper. Blend well.

Divide dough in half. Roll each half into a 12-inch square. Cut into four 6-inch squares. Place about ½ cup filling in the center of each square and moisten 2 adjacent sides with water. Fold remaining 2 sides across filling to form a triangle. Pinch edges to seal. Place on greased baking sheets. Slash tops of triangles to allow steam to escape. Bake in 350° oven for about 30 minutes or until done. Makes 8 small pasties.

HOT DOGS IN BLANKETS

1 lb. hot dogs	8 fresh bread slices
Pickle relish	8 slices bacon

Slit hot dogs lengthwise and fill with pickle relish. Cut crusts from bread and wrap a slice around each hot dog. Roll bacon around bread. Put on baking sheet and bake in 400° oven about 15 minutes. Makes 4 servings.

PIZZA DOGS

¼ c. onion, chopped
Dash garlic salt (optional)
2 T. vegetable oil
1 can condensed tomato soup
2 T. chopped parsley
¼ t. crushed dried oregano
8 hot dogs, slit lengthwise
8 rolls, split
6 oz. sliced mozzarella cheese

Sauté onion in oil until golden. Add ¼ cup water, soup, parsley and oregano. Bring to boil and simmer, stirring frequently, 15 minutes. Put a hot dog on each roll and arrange in large shallow baking pan. Cover hot dogs with tomato sauce and top with cheese. Put under broiler 1 minute, or until cheese is melted. Makes 8.

HOT DOGS WITH SAUERKRAUT

8 long thin hot dogs, partially split
   lengthwise
3 T. prepared mustard
8 T. butter, softened
8 rolls, partially split
¾ c. green pepper, slivered
¾ c. onion, chopped
1 lb. sauerkraut, undrained

Sauté hot dogs lightly until curled. Mix mustard with 6 tablespoons butter, spread on rolls and toast under broiler. Sauté next 2 ingredients lightly in remaining butter. Add sauerkraut and heat. Put a hot dog on each roll and top with sauerkraut. Makes 8.

CHEESE-TOPPED HOT DOGS IN ROLLS

6 hot dog rolls, split
   Prepared mustard
¼ c. soft butter
1 c. shredded sharp cheddar
2 egg whites, stiffly beaten
6 hot dogs

Spread inside of rolls with mustard. Cream butter and cheese until blended. Fold in egg whites. Split hot dogs lengthwise almost all the way through; put one into each roll and top with cheese mixture. Bake in 425° oven about 15 minutes. Makes 6.

HOT DOGS WITH ONION-CHILI SAUCE

1 c. onion, minced
2 cloves garlic, minced
¼ c. butter
½ t. salt
⅛ t. pepper
1½ T. Worcestershire
1½ T. prepared mustard
1½ t. sugar
½ c. chili sauce
1 lb. hot dogs
   Thick slices of Italian bread, toasted

Cook onion and garlic in the butter until golden. Add remaining ingredients except hot dogs and bread; heat. Split hot dogs lengthwise, put split side up in shallow pan and spoon sauce over them. Heat under broiler and serve between toasted bread slices topped with remaining sauce. Serves 4.

HOT DOGS IN BEER

1 lb. hot dogs	1 lg. carrot,
About 1½ c. beer	thinly sliced
1 lg. onion, sliced	½ t. Worcestershire

Put hot dogs in large saucepan and add enough beer to cover. Add remaining ingredients, bring to boil, lower heat and simmer 5 minutes. Remove hot dogs and serve on warm rolls. Makes 4 servings.

BEEF LOAF

2 lbs. ground beef
1 c. tomato sauce
1 egg
1 T. Worcestershire sauce
⅓ c. chopped green pepper
2 medium onions, chopped
¾ c. cracker crumbs, finely crushed
1 t. salt
¼ t. pepper
¼ c. catsup

Combine ground beef, tomato sauce, egg, Worcestershire sauce, green pepper, onions, cracker crumbs, salt and pepper. Mix lightly but thoroughly. Shape meat mixture into a 9 x 4 x 3-inch loaf and place on a rack in an open roasting pan. Bake in a 350° oven for 1 hour and 15 minutes. Pour catsup over top of beef loaf and continue baking 10 to 15 minutes or until done. Makes 6 to 8 servings.

SHEPHERD'S PIE (WITH ROAST)

2 c. mashed potatoes
2 c. cut up cooked roast beef, lamb, veal or pork
1 T. flour
2 T. fat or salad oil
  Leftover gravy
6 small onions, cooked and drained
1 c. carrots, cooked and quartered
1 c. cooked or canned peas, drained
1 egg, beaten

Grease 1½-quart casserole. Prepare mashed potatoes. In bowl lightly roll meat in flour until coated. In hot fat in skillet, brown meat lightly on all sides. Add 2½ cups leftover gravy (or as much as you have with hot water added to make 2½ cups.) Season to taste; thicken if necessary. Add onions, carrots, peas. Heat. Then pour into casserole. Fold egg into potatoes; arrange in ring on top of meat. Bake in a 425° oven for 10 to 15 minutes, until gravy bubbles and potato ring is light golden brown. Makes four servings.

You can also use lamb taken from a cold joint and put through a blender. Season well with herbs, onions, salt and pepper, and a few drops of Worcestershire sauce. Mix in a little good jellied stock—sufficient to moisten the meat throughout. Top with mashed potatoes beaten up with a little hot milk, butter, pepper and salt. Spread the potato crust evenly, and score with a knife. Bake in a hot oven until the surface is nicely browned and serve with stewed tomatoes.

BEEF CUBED STEAKS-TASTY TOPPING

4 beef cubed steaks
2 T. cooking fat
½ t. salt
¼ c. catsup
2 T. chopped green onion
¼ c. shredded cheddar cheese

Brown steaks on both sides in fat for 7 to 10 minutes. Pour off drippings. Top each steak with ⅛ teaspoon salt, 1 tablespoon catsup, 1½ teaspoons onion and 1 tablespoon shredded cheese. Cover and cook over low heat 2 to 3 minutes or until cheese melts. Makes 4 servings.

ALL-IN-A-POT LAMB ROAST

1 lamb leg, shank half (about 4 pounds)
2 onions, sliced thin
1 c. dry white wine
1 c. water
2 t. salt
1 t. rosemary
½ t. pepper
6 large carrots, quartered
1½ c. fresh mushrooms, sliced

Place lamb in small roasting pan that has a lid to fit. Add onion, wine, water, salt, rosemary and pepper. Cover roaster and bake at 325° for about one hour. Add carrots and mushrooms; cover and return to oven for another hour or until lamb and vegetables are tender. Remove lamb from oven and allow it to "rest" for about 10 minutes before carving. Cooking liquid may be skimmed of fat, strained and served with lamb and vegetables if desired. Makes 4 servings.

BARBECUED BEEF STRIPS

2 lbs. round steak (cut ½- to ¾-inch thick)
2 T. cooking fat
2 c. tomato sauce
⅓ c. water
2 T. brown sugar
1 T. prepared mustard
1 T. Worcestershire sauce
1 medium onion

Slice round steak in strips ⅛-inch thick or thinner and 3 to 4 inches long. Brown strips in fat. Pour off drippings. Combine tomato sauce, water, brown sugar, mustard and Worcestershire sauce. Add sauce and onion, thinly sliced. Stir to combine. Cover and cook slowly, stirring occasionally for 30 minutes or until meat is tender. Makes 6 to 8 servings.

BEEF KABOBS

1 steak, filet or sirloin, 1-inch thick
 (2 to 3 lbs.)
½ c. red wine
1 T. wine vinegar
¼ c. olive oil
1 t. Worcestershire sauce
1 T. chopped fresh tarragon
1 clove garlic, crushed
½ t. salt
¼ t. pepper
4 onions, quartered
2 green peppers, cut lengthwise
 in eighths
4 tomatoes, quartered

Prepare 8 long skewers. Cut steak into 1-inch cubes. Mix wine, wine vinegar, oil, Worcestershire sauce, tarragon, garlic, salt and pepper in a bowl. Stir meat into marinade and marinate for 1 to 24 hours. Place meat on skewers, alternating with vegetables. Pour marinade into a large flat baking pan (jelly roll pan). Place skewers in marinade so that vegetables and meat will rest in seasoning. This may be prepared well in advance. Skewers should be grilled over a hot fire about 3 to 4 inches over coals so that vegetables have a chance to cook without charring. Turn skewers frequently. Kabobs should take no more than 10 minutes. Serves 4.

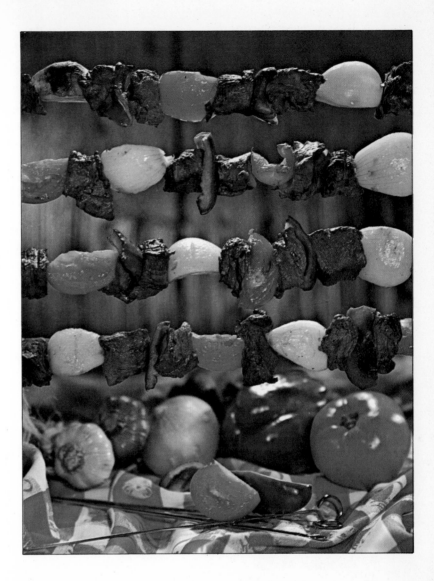

SHEPHERD'S PIE

1 lb. ground beef chuck
¼ c. chopped green pepper
¼ c. chopped onion
1 T. shortening
1 T. flour
1 t. salt
½ t. chili powder
 Dash pepper
½ c. tomato ketchup
1 c. water
1½ to 2 c. mixed vegetables, cooked and
 drained
3 c. seasoned hot mashed potatoes
 Paprika

Sauté ground beef, green pepper and onion in shortening until meat is browned and green pepper is tender. Drain off any excess fat. Sprinkle in four next ingredients; stir in ketchup, water and cooked vegetables. Combine well and cook until mixture thickens. Divide mixture into six 10-ounce baking dishes or one 2-quart casserole. Top with potatoes and sprinkle with paprika. Place under broiler to brown; or bake in preheated 425° oven for 15 minutes. Makes six servings.

Sausage, so familiar in country kitchens, was popular over a thousand years B.C. Sausage-eating was a popular pastime in ancient Rome. In fact, many of their feasts centered around sausage. The Romans called it "salus," meaning salted or preserved meat.

Early American settlers found the Indians making sausage. They preserved a combination of chopped, dried meat with dried berries. Sausage-making skills came to the New World with each ethnic group. Old family recipes once shared freely in country kitchens became closely guarded secrets. Old World specialties blended with new taste preferences.

In all likelihood, no two sausage makers will agree on ingredients. Still, regional sausage recipes make outstanding country kitchen dishes.

SAUSAGEBURGERS

2 lbs. pork sausage
3 T. water
2 large tomatoes, each cut into 4 slices
1 medium-sized onion, cut into 8 slices
   and separated into rings
8 hamburger buns, warmed

Shape sausage into 8 patties, ½- to ¾-inch thick and 3 to 4 inches in diameter. Place in a cold frying pan, add water, cover and cook over low heat for 5 minutes. Pour off drippings. Cook patties slowly on both sides until well-done. Place patties, tomato slices and onion rings between halves of warmed hamburger buns. Makes 8 sandwiches.

SURPRISE SAUSAGE 'N EGGS

1 lb. bulk pork sausage meat
½ c. oatmeal (quick or old-fashioned, uncooked)
1 egg
¼ c. milk
4 hard-cooked eggs

Combine sausage, oats, egg and milk. Mix thoroughly. Divide meat mixture into four parts and shape each part around a hard-cooked egg. Place eggs on a rack in a shallow baking pan. Bake in a preheated 375° oven about 35 minutes or until sausage is cooked. Makes 4 servings.

SAUSAGE-CORN BREAD PIE

1 lb. fresh pork sausage
1 c. yellow cornmeal
1 c. flour
¼ c. sugar
4 t. baking powder
1 egg
1 c. milk

Brown pork sausage, separating it into pieces. Pour off drippings, reserving ¼ cup. Sift together cornmeal, flour, sugar and baking powder. Add egg, milk and ¼ cup pork sausage drippings. Mix to combine thoroughly. Fold in sausage. Turn batter into a greased 9-inch pie plate. Bake in a 425° oven for 25 minutes or until done. Makes 6 servings.

SAUSAGE-MACARONI GOULASH

1 lb. pork sausage links
1 c. chopped green pepper
1 c. chopped onion
3½ c. stewed tomatoes, undrained
1 c. elbow macaroni, uncooked
1 t. salt
¼ t. pepper
1 T. thick steak sauce
1 c. dairy sour cream
Chopped parsley

Halve sausages crosswise. Sauté in large skillet until nicely browned. Remove. Drain off all but 3 tablespoons fat from skillet. In hot fat, sauté green pepper and onion, stirring, about 5 minutes. Add sausages, tomatoes, macaroni, salt, pepper and steak sauce; bring to boiling. Reduce heat; simmer, covered, 30 minutes, stirring occasionally. Remove from heat. Stir in sour cream, mixing well. Sprinkle with parsley. Makes 4 servings.

BEEF CASSEROLE

- 2 lbs. round steak, cut in ½-inch cubes
- 3 T. fat
- 1 large onion, chopped
- 1 clove garlic, finely chopped
- 2 T. flour
- ¾ c. canned mushrooms and broth
- ½ c. chopped celery
- 1 c. thick sour cream
- 1 c. tomato sauce
- 1 t. salt
- ⅛ t. pepper
- 1 T. Worcestershire sauce

Brown meat in hot fat. Add onion and garlic and cook until golden. Stir in flour slowly. Add remaining ingredients and mix well. Turn into greased 3-quart casserole. Bake, uncovered, in 325° oven until meat is tender, about 1½ hours. Serves 6.

SPANISH RICE

- 1 lb. ground beef
- 4 t. butter
- 1 c. chopped onion
- 1 green pepper, chopped
- ¼ c. diced celery
- 2 c. stewed tomatoes
- 2 t. salt
- ⅛ t. black pepper
- 3 c. hot cooked rice
  Chopped parsley

Brown ground beef in butter. Add onions, green pepper and celery and simmer on range top until almost tender. Pour into ovenproof casserole (4 quarts or larger). Mix in tomatoes, salt, pepper and rice. Blend well. Garnish top with chopped parsley. Bake in 350° oven for 30 minutes. Serves eight.

PORK AND TOM...

- 2 pork blade steaks, c...
- 1 large onion, choppe...
- 3½ c. stewed tomatoes
- 1 T. sugar
- 1½ t. salt
- ⅛ t. pepper
- ⅛ t. thyme
- 8 slices bread, toasted
- 4 oz. sliced cheese, if desired

Cut pork steaks into strips ½-inch wide and 3 inches long. Cook pork strips and onion slowly in large frying pan, stirring until lightly browned. Add tomatoes, sugar, salt, pepper and thyme and stir to combine, breaking up tomatoes. Cut slices of toast into 1-inch squares and place in 13 x 9-inch baking dish. Pour meat mixture over toast squares, distributing evenly. Cut cheese slices into 1-inch squares and place on top. Cover securely and bake in a 350° oven for 35 minutes. Remove cover and bake 10 minutes longer. Makes 6 servings.

MACARONI AND CHEESE BAKE

- 1 c. uncooked elbow macaroni
- 2 c. corn flakes
- ¼ c. butter, melted
- 3 T. finely chopped onion
- 1 10¾-oz. can (1¼ cups) condensed cream of mushroom soup
- ⅓ c. milk
- 1¼ c. (5 oz.) grated sharp cheddar cheese

Cook macaroni according to package directions. Drain, rinse and set aside. Measure corn flakes; crush into fine crumbs. Mix crumbs with 2 tablespoons of the melted butter. Set crumb mixture aside for topping. Place remaining melted butter and onion in medium-sized saucepan; cook over low heat until tender. Stir in soup, milk and cheese; cook just until cheese is melted, stirring occasionally. Remove from heat. Place cooked macaroni in buttered 8 x 8 x 2-inch (1-quart) baking dish; pour hot cheese sauce over top. Stir to combine. Sprinkle evenly with crumb mixture. Bake in 350° oven about 30 minutes or until thoroughly heated. Makes 4 servings.

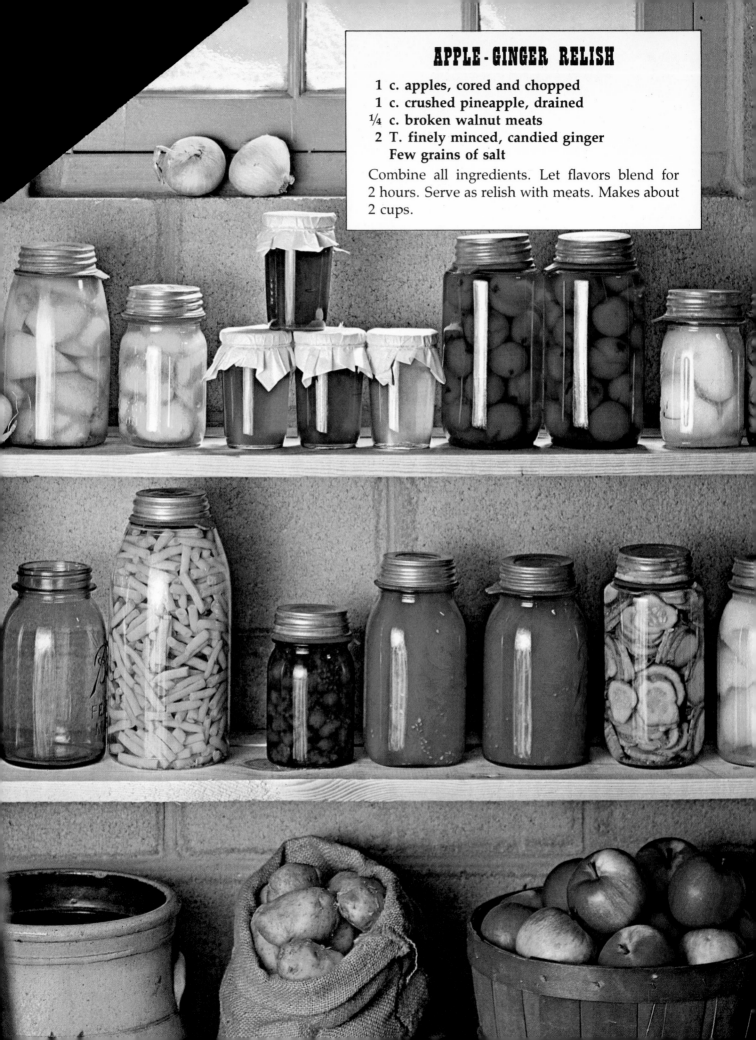

APPLE-GINGER RELISH

1 c. apples, cored and chopped
1 c. crushed pineapple, drained
¼ c. broken walnut meats
2 T. finely minced, candied ginger
Few grains of salt

Combine all ingredients. Let flavors blend for 2 hours. Serve as relish with meats. Makes about 2 cups.

ACCOMPANIMENTS

DILLY CARROTS

8 medium carrots,
   cut into sticks
½ c. water
¼ c. cider vinegar

1 t. tarragon
1 t. dill weed
1 t. seasoned salt

Place all ingredients in a saucepan. Bring to a boil; cover and reduce heat. Simmer 30 minutes or until tender-crisp. Chill several hours or overnight. Great as a snack, hors d'oeuvre, or salad.

CORN RELISH

8 c. corn, boiled and cut from cob
4 c. chopped cabbage
1 c. chopped sweet green pepper
1 c. chopped sweet red pepper
2 large onions, chopped.
1 c. sugar
2 T. ground mustard
1 T. mustard seed
1 T. salt
1 T. celery seed
4 c. cider vinegar
1 c. water

Combine all ingredients in large, heavy kettle. Simmer 20 minutes. You may add more sugar and salt to taste. Pack, boiling hot, into sterilized jars, leaving ½-inch headspace. Adjust caps. Process 10 minutes in boiling water bath. Makes about 6 pints.

APPLE BUTTER

Wash and quarter enough apples to fill a 16-quart kettle. Add 2 cups of water. Cook slowly over very low heat and stir constantly. Use a heavy kettle with a broad, flat bottom to allow the apples to bubble freely. When they are thoroughly cooked, cool slightly. Run through a food mill. There should be about 8 quarts of pulp.

Measure 2 cups of sugar to 4 cups of apple pulp. Place mixture back in a heavy kettle. Here again the broad, flat kettle bottom is necessary to allow the sugar and pulp to mix and cook freely. Use a wooden spoon or a flat paddle to stir the mixture constantly while it is cooking over a very low heat. The stirring allows the steam to escape and prevents scorching. Add 10 2-inch sticks of cinnamon. Check for doneness by placing some apple butter on a cool saucer. If no rim of liquid forms around the edge of the butter, it is ready for the jar. Place in hot sterilized jars. Seal at once. Makes about 12 pints.

PEACH CHUTNEY

1 29-oz. can sliced
   cling peaches
1 c. sugar
¾ c. vinegar
1 c. pitted prunes
⅓ c. chopped candied
   ginger

1 clove garlic,
   minced
½ t. curry powder
¼ t. cinnamon
¼ t. ground cloves
⅓ c. chopped almonds

Drain peaches, reserving syrup. In large saucepan, combine syrup with remaining ingredients except nuts and peaches. Bring to a boil; reduce heat and simmer, stirring frequently, for 45 minutes. Add nuts and peaches. Pour into sterilized jars and seal tightly. Cool and store in dark place. Makes 8 cups.

END-OF-THE-GARDEN PICKLES

1 c. sliced cucumbers
1 c. chopped sweet peppers
1 c. chopped cabbage
1 c. sliced onions
1 c. chopped green tomatoes
1 c. chopped carrots
1 c. green beans, cut in 1-inch pieces
1 c. chopped celery
2 T. mustard seed
1 T. celery seed
2 c. cider vinegar
2 c. sugar
2 T. turmeric

Combine cucumbers, peppers, cabbage, onions and tomatoes in large container. Soak in salt brine (½ cup salt to 2 quarts cold water) overnight. Drain well. Combine and cook the carrots and green beans until tender. Drain well. Mix all vegetables together with remaining ingredients. Boil 10 minutes. Pack into hot, sterilized jars. Adjust caps. Process 10 minutes in boiling water bath. Makes about 6 pints.

No picnic basket should leave a country kitchen without some pickled eggs. This old-fashioned method of preserving eggs offers a country cook a unique economical source of protein to serve with her picnic lunch.

Pickled eggs can be kept up to several months in the pickling solution at refrigerator temperatures. It is a good idea to check the refrigerated pickled eggs often as their spicy flavor becomes too pronounced for some tastes.

DEVILED EGGS

6 pickled eggs	2 t. lemon juice
1 t. Worcestershire sauce	or vinegar
	1/8 t. ground pepper
3/4 t. salad mustard	3 T. mayonnaise
1/2 t. salt	or salad dressing

Cut eggs in half. Remove yolks and press through sieve. Combine yolks with remaining ingredients; beat until smooth. If desired add more seasoning and salad dressing. Refill whites with fork, spoon or pastry tube. Makes 12 stuffed halves.

RED BEET EGGS

1 t. dried mustard	1 1-lb. can
2 T. sugar	baby beets
1 t. salt	4 hard-boiled eggs
1/2 c. cider vinegar	

Mix together mustard, sugar, salt and vinegar and cook to the boiling point. Pour over well-drained beets and set aside to cool. When cool, add the shelled hard-boiled eggs and refrigerate overnight. Shake container occasionally so eggs will pick up the beet color all over. Serve beets as a salad on water cress. The pickled eggs may be used to garnish a salad or served separately. Makes four servings.

DARK AND SPICY EGGS

1 1/2 c. cider vinegar
1/2 c. water
1 T. dark brown sugar
2 t. granulated sugar
1 t. mixed pickling spice
1/4 t. liquid smoke or hickory smoke salt
2 t. salt
1 doz. hard-boiled eggs, peeled

Combine all ingredients except eggs, heat to near boiling and simmer for five minutes. Pour the solution over the hard-boiled eggs in a quart jar or other suitable container which can be sealed tightly. Seal and immediately store in the refrigerator to season.

DILLED EGGS

1 1/2 c. white vinegar	1/4 t. mustard seed
1 c. water	1/2 t. onion juice
3/4 t. dill seed	1/2 t. minced garlic
1/4 t. white pepper	1 doz. hard-boiled eggs, peeled
3 t. salt	

Combine all ingredients but eggs in saucepan. Bring to boiling over medium heat. Boil for five minutes. Pour the pickling solution over the hard-cooked eggs in a quart jar or larger container. Seal and refrigerate. Season for one week.

PICKLED EGGS WITH CARAWAY SEED

8 eggs	2 c. cider vinegar
2 T. sugar	8 black peppers
1 t. salt	3 to 4 whole cloves
1 bud garlic	2 t. caraway seed

Hard-boil eggs; remove shells and cool. Put eggs in jar with a tight cover. In a pan combine above ingredients and bring to boiling. Cook slowly 20 to 25 minutes. Strain and pour boiling mixture over cold eggs. Cover tightly. Store at least two days before using.

BEST-OF-ALL CHILI SAUCE

1½ t. ground nutmeg
1½ t. ground allspice
1½ t. ground cloves
½ t. ginger
1 dried hot red pepper
7 lbs. peeled tomatoes
3 c. onions
2 large sweet green peppers
1½ T. salt
3 c. chopped celery
2 c. cider vinegar
1½ c. granulated sugar
1½ sticks cinnamon

Combine first 5 ingredients in cheesecloth bag. Chop tomatoes, onions, celery and peppers fine. Add remaining ingredients. Bring to a boil on range top. Then place pan in a 350° oven for 2 to 3 hours, stirring occasionally during the last hour of cooking. When sauce reaches desired consistency, pour into sterilized jars and seal at once. Makes 5 to 6 pints.

Some folks claim you can find a little bit of heaven when you step into a country kitchen when the catsup kettle is brewing. The tangy combination of tomatoes, onions and green peppers with a floating spice bag releases a heady draft of steam each time the wooden spoon makes its path through the thickening broth.

Call it what you will—catsup, catchup, or ketchup—this nippy condiment is a favorite with young and old alike.

Catsup or sauces may be made of either fruits or vegetables. The main difference between the two is that catsup is strained through a fine sieve, while the sauce is left unstrained. Both are boiled to a thick liquid stage.

Pioneer cooks made catsup from any number of ingredients including apples, grapes, walnuts, mushrooms, currants, cranberries and gooseberries. Still it is the classic tomato catsup we know best today.

TOMATO CATSUP

1 peck (12½ lbs.) ripe tomatoes
3 large onions
¼ t. cayenne pepper
2 c. cider vinegar
1½ T. broken stick cinnamon
1 T. whole cloves
3 cloves garlic (finely chopped)
1 T. paprika
1 c. sugar
2½ t. salt

Wash and slice tomatoes and boil about 15 minutes or until soft. Slice the onions into another kettle. Cover with a small quantity of water and cook until tender. Run the cooked onions and tomatoes through a sieve. Mix the onion and tomato pulp. Add the cayenne pepper. Boil this mixture rapidly until it has been reduced to about ½ of its original volume.

Meanwhile place vinegar in an enamel pan; add a spice bag containing the cinnamon, cloves and garlic. Allow this to simmer for about 30 minutes. Then bring to boiling point. Place cover on pan and remove from heat. Allow this to stand in covered pan until ready to use.

When tomato mixture has cooked down to ½ original volume, add vinegar mixture, which should measure 1½ cups. Add the paprika, sugar and salt and boil rapidly for 10 minutes or until desired consistency is reached. Pour while boiling hot into sterilized jars and seal at once.

BLENDER CATSUP

48 medium tomatoes (about 8 lbs.)
2 ripe sweet red peppers
2 sweet green peppers
4 onions
3 T. salt
1½ t. allspice
3 t. dry mustard
3 c. white vinegar
3 c. sugar
1½ t. cloves
1½ t. cinnamon
½ t. hot red pepper

Quarter tomatoes; remove stem ends. Add peppers, seeded and cut in strips, and onions, peeled and quartered. Mix. Put vegetables in blender container, filling jar ¾ full. Blend at high speed 4 seconds; pour into large kettle. Repeat until all vegetables are blended. Add vinegar, sugar, salt and spices, tied loosely in thin muslin bag. Simmer, uncovered, in 325° oven or in electric saucepan until volume is reduced one-half. Remove spices. Seal immediately in hot sterilized jars. Makes five pints.

CRANBERRY RIBBON SALAD

1 1-lb. can whole cranberry sauce
2 T. lemon juice
½ pt. cream, whipped
¼ c. confectioners' sugar
1 t. vanilla
¾ c. chopped hickory nuts

Add lemon juice to cranberry sauce. Pour into freezing tray. Combine whipped cream, sugar, vanilla and nuts. Spoon whipped cream mixture over cranberry layer and freeze. When ready to serve, slice and place each piece on crisp lettuce.

TANGERINE-CRANBERRY RELISH

1 lb. fresh or frozen cranberries
4 medium tangerines
1½ to 2 c. sugar
2 c. seedless raisins or nuts, coarsely chopped

Wash cranberries (do not thaw frozen berries) and put through the medium blade of food chopper. Wash tangerines; remove peel. Put the peel through food chopper. Remove seeds from tangerines and cut sections into small pieces. Combine cranberries, tangerine peel and pieces, and sugar; stir until sugar is dissolved. Add raisins or nuts, blend well and turn into glass jars. Cover and refrigerate. Relish will keep for several weeks. Makes 2½ pints.

HOT CRANBERRY BUTTER

2 c. cranberries   ½ c. water
  (fresh or frozen)   ¼ c. brown sugar
1 c. granulated sugar   ¼ c. butter

Combine cranberries, granulated sugar and water in saucepan. Heat to boiling, stirring until sugar dissolves. Boil until berries pop (about 5 minutes). Add brown sugar and butter. Heat until dissolved. Serve hot with French toast, waffles or pancakes.

CRANBERRY-APPLE CIDER

1 lb. fresh or frozen cranberries
1 c. sweet cider
2 tart apples with skins, sliced
1 c. honey
  Grated rind of 1 lemon
  Pinch of ground mace

Simmer the cranberries, cider and apples gently until fruit is soft. Add honey, rind and mace. Simmer for 5 minutes. Cool. Serve with meat, fowl or fish. Makes 2 pints.

MOLASSES CRANBERRY SHERBET

1 envelope   2½ c. water
  unflavored gelatin   1½ c. sugar
½ c. cold water   ⅓ c. molasses
4 c. fresh or   ¼ c. lemon juice
  frozen cranberries

Soften gelatin in one-half cup water. Cook cranberries, covered, in the two and one-half cups water until skins break open. Put cranberries through sieve. Combine cranberries, sugar, molasses and gelatin. Cook over medium heat, stirring constantly, until sugar and gelatin dissolve. Remove from heat. Stir in lemon juice. Cool. Pour into an eight-inch square pan. Freeze until firm. Turn into chilled bowl and let stand until slightly softened. Beat until thick and mushy. Pour into pan and freeze until firm. Makes about one and one-half quarts.

CRANBERRY-ORANGE HONEY

1 1-lb. can whole cranberry sauce
¼ c. orange juice
2 to 3 T. honey

Mix cranberry sauce, orange juice and honey to suit your "sweet tooth." Delightful sauce with pancakes. Makes 2 cups.

CIDER SAUCE

2 T. quick-cooking tapioca	¼ t. salt
	1½ c. cider
¼ c. sugar	1 T. butter

Combine tapioca, sugar, salt and cider in saucepan. Let stand 5 minutes. Cook and stir over medium heat until mixture comes to boil; remove from heat; stir in butter. Cool 15 to 20 minutes; stir. Serve warm on plain cake, gingerbread or ice cream. Makes about 1⅔ cups sauce.

HOT MULLED CIDER

½ c. brown sugar	1 t. whole cloves
¼ t. salt	3-inch cinnamon
2 qts. cider	sticks
1 t. whole allspice	Dash nutmeg

Combine brown sugar, salt and cider. Tie spices in small cheesecloth bag; add to cider mixture. Slowly bring to boil; simmer, covered, about 20 minutes. Use cinnamon stick as muddlers. Makes 10 servings.

BOILED CIDER PIE

8-inch shallow pastry shell, baked
⅓ c. grated maple sugar (or brown sugar)
⅓ c. boiled cider
3 eggs, separated
½ t. nutmeg
1 t. butter
½ c. seeded raisins
⅓ c. granulated sugar

Dissolve maple sugar by heating with boiled cider. Add beaten egg yolks very slowly, stirring constantly; cook until thickened. Add nutmeg, butter and raisins. Pour into baked shell. Cover with meringue made from egg whites and granulated sugar. Bake in 325° oven about 15 minutes, or until meringue is a delicate, golden brown.

CIDER SAUCE FOR PUDDING

2 T. butter	1 c. cider
1 c. brown sugar, packed	¼ c. raisins
	Nutmeg
2 T. flour	

Melt butter in saucepan. Gradually add the combined brown sugar and flour, stirring constantly. Add cider; bring to boil, and let thicken just a little. Remove from heat. Add raisins. Pour into small pitcher or serving bowl and sprinkle with nutmeg. Serve hot with bread, cottage, or plain steamed pudding, or white cake. Note: If sauce becomes too thick, thin with cold cider.

SPICED CIDER

1 qt. cider	1 stick cinnamon
1 lemon, sliced thinly	1 whole nutmeg, crushed
Peel of 1 orange and 1 lemon	6 cloves
	1 T. sugar

In a large saucepan, mix cider, fruit and peels, spices, and sugar. Bring just to a boil. Immediately turn down heat and let cider simmer for 10 minutes. Strain and serve hot.

If you prefer, make this recipe a day ahead. Keep it chilled in the refrigerator and reheat just before serving. Garnish with lemon slices and cinnamon sticks.

CIDER GELATIN SALAD

1 T. unflavored gelatin	¼ c. sugar
	1¾ c. hot cider
2 T. cold water	1½ c. diced apple
2 T. lemon juice	½ c. diced celery

Soften gelatin in combined cold water and lemon juice. Dissolve sugar in hot cider. Add softened gelatin; stir until dissolved. Chill. When mixture begins to set, stir in apple and celery. Turn into 6 wet individual molds; chill. Unmold; serve on lettuce and top with mayonnaise and sprinkling of chopped nuts. Makes 6 servings.

VEGETABLES

ASPARAGUS WITH WATER CHESTNUT SAUCE

- ¼ c. butter
- 5 T. flour
- 2 t. salt
- ¼ t. pepper
- 2¼ c. milk
- 3 T. lemon juice
- 2 T. cubed sharp cheddar cheese
- ½ c. thinly sliced water chestnuts
- 2 lbs. fresh asparagus spears, cooked

Melt butter in saucepan. Stir in flour and seasonings. Gradually add milk and lemon juice. Cook over low heat, stirring constantly, until mixture thickens. Stir in cheddar cheese and water chestnuts. Arrange asparagus on platter. Spoon sauce over asparagus. Garnish with strips of lemon rind. Makes 6 to 8 servings.

CREAM OF ASPARAGUS SOUP

- ¾ c. water
- ¾ t. salt
- 1 lb. fresh asparagus, cut in pieces (about 2½ c.)
- 1 c. light cream
- 2 T. butter

In saucepan, heat water and salt to boiling. Add asparagus; cover and simmer 8 to 10 minutes, till asparagus is just tender. Put asparagus and cooking water into blender container; cover and blend on low speed till asparagus is finely chopped. Add cream and blend on high speed till smooth. Return soup to saucepan; add butter and heat through. If desired, dot each serving with additional butter. Makes 4 servings.

ASPARAGUS CASSEROLE

- 1 lb. fresh asparagus, cooked and drained
- ½ lb. fresh mushrooms, sliced and lightly sautéed
- 2 T. butter
- 2 T. regular flour
- ¾ t. seasoned salt
- ¼ t. freshly ground pepper
  Few grains paprika
- 1 c. cream
- ½ c. shredded Swiss cheese
- ½ c. very finely cut celery
  Round scalloped crackers, crushed

Heat butter in a saucepan. Stir in flour and seasonings; cook until mixture bubbles. Add cream gradually, stirring until blended. Bring rapidly to boiling; cook and stir 1 to 2 minutes. Remove from heat; add cheese and stir until cheese is melted. Mix in mushrooms and celery. Line the bottom of a greased shallow 1½-quart casserole with half the asparagus. Pour sauce over asparagus and arrange the remaining asparagus on top. Sprinkle with cracker crumbs. Bake at 350° for 25 minutes or until thoroughly heated. If desired, place under broiler until crumbs are browned. Makes 6 servings.

SWEET 'N SOUR ASPARAGUS SALAD

- 1 lb. fresh asparagus spears
- 6 slices bacon
- ¼ c. wine vinegar
- 2 t. sugar
  Dash salt
  Dash pepper
- 2 green onions, finely chopped (about 2 t.)
  Shredded lettuce
- 2 hard-boiled eggs, sliced

Cook asparagus in boiling salted water 8 to 10 minutes or until tender; drain. Meanwhile, cook bacon in skillet till crisp. Remove bacon, drain and crumble and set aside. Add vinegar, sugar, salt, pepper and onion to bacon drippings in skillet. Add asparagus; heat through. Arrange a bed of lettuce in each of 6 salad bowls. Remove asparagus from skillet; arrange on lettuce. Top with egg slices. Pour hot bacon dressing over each salad. Sprinkle with bacon. Makes 6 servings.

BAKED BEANS WITH TOMATOES

2½ c. dried navy beans
1 medium onion, sliced
3 oz. salt pork, sliced
2 c. canned tomatoes, sieved
2 c. water
1 t. salt
⅛ t. dry mustard
Few grains cayenne
⅓ c. brown sugar, packed

Wash beans thoroughly and put them into a 3-quart bowl. Add enough water to come 2 inches above beans and soak overnight. Next morning drain and combine with the next 7 ingredients in a saucepan; bring to boil, reduce heat, cover and simmer 1 hour or until beans are soft enough to break open. Turn into a buttered casserole or baking dish and add brown sugar. Pull slices of salt pork to the top, cover and bake 2 hours in a 250° oven. Remove cover and bake another hour. Serve hot. Makes 5 servings.

LIMA BAKE

1½ c. dried lima beans
½ c. chopped onion
½ t. salt
1 c. chopped celery
¼ c. chopped green pepper
2 c. stewed tomatoes
¼ t. hot pepper sauce
4 slices bacon

Soak beans in cold water for 8 hours or overnight. Drain well. Place limas in large kettle; cover with water and bring to boil. Add onion and salt. Lower heat and let simmer slowly until beans are tender, about 30 minutes. Drain beans well, reserving ¼ cup liquid. Combine limas, celery, green pepper, tomatoes, hot pepper sauce and reserved lima liquid in 2½-quart casserole. Bake uncovered at 350° about 1 hour or until vegetables are tender. Meanwhile, fry bacon to desired doneness. Arrange bacon as desired on top of casserole before serving. Makes 4 to 6 servings.

COUNTRY BAKED BEANS

2 c. dried Great Northern Beans
6 slices bacon or salt pork
2 T. chopped onion
1 t. salt
⅛ t. pepper
4 T. molasses
3 T. brown sugar
1 t. dry mustard
2 c. hot water
3 T. tomato soup
2 T. catsup

Soak beans overnight. Drain. Brown meat in heavy skillet until golden brown. Put into bean pot. Add chopped onion and stir. Add beans, salt, pepper, molasses, sugar, mustard and water. Stir. Add tomato soup, catsup and enough additional water to cover the beans. Cover the bean pot. Bake 6 to 8 hours at 250°. Add water as needed to keep the beans moist. Uncover the last hour of baking so that the beans brown. Serves 4 or 5.

BOSTON BAKED BEANS

4 c. navy beans
½ lb. fat salt pork
2 t. salt
1½ T. brown sugar
¼ c. molasses
½ t. dry mustard

Wash and pick over beans. Soak overnight in cold water. In the morning, drain, cover with fresh water and simmer until skins break; turn into bean pot. Score pork and press into beans, leaving ¼ inch above the beans. Add salt, sugar, molasses and mustard. Add boiling water to cover. Cover and bake in 250° oven for about 8 hours without stirring, adding water as necessary to keep beans covered. Uncover during last half hour to brown. Serves 8.

HOME-BAKED BEANS

2 c. navy beans
½ lb. fat bacon, sliced
1½ t. salt
½ t. pepper
¼ c. brown sugar
1½ t. dry mustard
1 medium onion, quartered

Wash beans, cover with water and soak overnight. Cook slowly until skins burst or until just tender. Drain, reserving liquid. Place half the beans in bean pot. Bury part of bacon in beans and add half of combined remaining ingredients. Add remaining beans and seasonings. Place remaining bacon over top. Cover with bean liquid. Cover and bake at 250° to 300° for 6 to 8 hours. If necessary, add more liquid. Serves 6 to 8.

Tomatoes have an interesting history. Intrigued by the bright South American fruit, Spanish explorers took seeds back to Europe. But Europeans soon developed superstitions about the member of the deadly nightshade family.

Some thought them poisonous or a powerful drug. Others grew the plants as curiosities. Rumors that the tomato stimulated love earned it the name "love apple."

This superstition traveled to the colonies, where it was said that Thomas Jefferson was one of the first to try the fruit.

While some folks take the tomato for granted, country cooks know it is a food for all seasons. You will find it in everything from sauces, soups, stews, casseroles, baked dishes and salads to preserves, cakes, dinner drinks and country kitchen snacks.

STUFFED TOMATO SALAD

5 large tomatoes, chilled
  Crisp lettuce
2 c. creamed cottage cheese
1 T. chopped chives
  Paprika

Wash tomatoes and remove core from stem ends. Cut into 6 sections, leaving bottom attached; then open sections out like petals. Place on salad plates in nests of lettuce. Mix cottage cheese with chives. Pile into centers of tomatoes and sprinkle tops lightly with paprika. Makes 5 servings.

MOLDED TOMATO RELISH

2 c. canned stewed tomatoes
1 3-oz. pkg. lemon gelatin
½ t. salt
1 T. vinegar

Pour tomatoes into saucepan, saving can to use as a mold. Bring tomatoes to a boil. Reduce heat and simmer 2 minutes. Add gelatin, salt and vinegar; stir until gelatin is dissolved. Pour into can. Chill until firm, about 4 hours. To unmold, dip can in warm water and puncture bottom of can. Makes about 2 cups or 6 servings.

TOMATO AND CUCUMBER SALAD

5 tomatoes, sliced
¼ c. salad oil
¼ c. cider vinegar
1 T. chopped parsley
  Fresh dill, minced
3 fresh green onions,
  finely chopped
1 small head of lettuce
3 cucumbers, peeled
  and sliced
  Salt and pepper

Combine the tomatoes, oil, vinegar, parsley, dill and green onions in a large bowl. Refrigerate 2 hours. To serve: Shred lettuce in large salad bowl. Arrange tomato mixture and cucumbers on top of lettuce. Season with salt and pepper to taste. Toss lightly to blend. Serve. Makes 6 to 8 servings.

TOMATO AND ZUCCHINI CASSEROLE

2 c. sliced zucchini (about ½ lb.)
1 c. (1 medium) onion, thinly sliced
2 small tomatoes, sliced
⅓ c. fine, dry bread crumbs
  Salt
  Pepper
½ c. cheddar cheese, grated
1 tomato, cut in wedges

In a 1½-quart casserole, layer half each of the zucchini, onions, sliced tomatoes, and bread crumbs, sprinkling liberally with salt and pepper. Repeat layers. Top with tomato wedges. Cover and bake one hour in 375° oven. Uncover and sprinkle with cheese. Return to oven until cheese melts. Makes 6 servings.

BAKED EGG AND TOMATO

4 large slices tomato
  Salt and pepper to taste
4 eggs

Put tomato slices in separate greased custard cups. Sprinkle with salt and pepper. Drop egg in each. Bake in 350° oven until eggs are set. Serve on buttered toast. Serves 4.

PENNSYLVANIA DUTCH SPINACH

4 slices bacon, diced
3 c. chopped raw spinach
3 T. flour
1¼ c. hot water
2 T. sugar
1 T. cider vinegar
1 t. salt
⅛ t. pepper
2 hard-cooked eggs

Fry bacon until crisp; add bacon to spinach. Add flour to drippings and blend. Add hot water and cook over low heat until thick, stirring constantly. Add sugar, vinegar and seasonings. Pour over spinach. Stir well until wilted and garnish with sliced, hard-cooked eggs. Serves 6.

SPINACH SOUFFLÉ

3 c. fresh chopped spinach
3 T. butter
3 T. flour
1½ c. milk or cream
½ t. sugar
Salt to taste
Pepper to taste
Dash of nutmeg
Garlic powder to taste
Buttered bread crumbs

Cook spinach 5 minutes. Drain. Melt butter over low heat. Stir in flour until well mixed. Gradually add milk and continue stirring until thoroughly blended. Cook over low heat until thickened, stirring constantly. Season with sugar, salt, pepper, nutmeg and garlic powder. Add spinach and mix well. Turn into buttered casserole. Top with bread crumbs. Bake at 350° for about 25 minutes, or until bread crumbs are browned and casserole is bubbly.

WILTED SPINACH TOSS

3 slices bacon
¼ c. vinegar
1 T. salad oil
1½ t. sugar
¼ t. salt
⅛ t. dried tarragon leaves, crushed
Dash freshly ground black pepper
¼ c. chopped celery
1 T. sliced green onion
6 c. torn fresh spinach (about ½ lb.)
2 medium oranges, peeled and cut in bite-size pieces

In large skillet, cook bacon till crisp; drain, reserving 2 tablespoons drippings. Crumble bacon and set aside. Stir vinegar, oil, sugar, salt, tarragon and pepper into reserved drippings; bring to a boil. Add chopped celery and sliced green onion. Gradually add spinach, tossing just till leaves are coated and wilted slightly. Add oranges and crumbled bacon; toss lightly. Makes 6 to 8 servings.

CREAMED SPINACH

4 T. butter	**1 c. milk**
1 large onion, chopped	**½ t. nutmeg**
	¼ t. allspice
2 lbs. fresh spinach	**1 t. salt**
2 T. flour	**¼ t. pepper**

Melt 2 tablespoons butter in large saucepan. Sauté onion in butter until brown. Add washed, drained spinach to onion and cook, covered, for 3 to 5 minutes. Drain and chop. Return spinach to saucepan. While spinach is cooking, work remaining butter and flour together with a fork. When spinach is cooked, lower heat and add butter/flour mixture a little at a time until it is all smoothly incorporated. Add milk and seasonings. Reheat. Use as a garnish with other vegetables. Serves 6.

BOILED CORN ON THE COB

Place cleaned corn on the cob into a large kettle. Cover with cold water. Omit salt; it tends to toughen the corn. Bring just to a boil and then let the ears stand in boiling water for 1 minute. Eat at once with plenty of soft butter and salt to taste.

PARSLEY BUTTER

Mix ¼ cup softened butter, 2 tablespoons each chopped parsley and green onion, ½ teaspoon salt and a dash of pepper.

ROASTED CORN ON THE COB

Remove outer husks and silks, but leave a complete covering of inner husks. Soak in salted water for about 30 minutes. Wrap each ear tightly in foil and place on gray, glowing coals for about 15 minutes. Turn frequently. Remove the foil and husks. Serve with melted butter and pastry brushes.

CARROT-STUFFED BAKED POTATOES

- 4 baking potatoes
- 1 c. mashed cooked carrots
- 2 T. grated onion
- 1½ t. salt
- ¼ t. dried dill weed
- ⅛ t. pepper
- 3 T. milk
- 2 T. butter
- 1 egg

Scrub potatoes well. Dry potatoes and prick with fork. Bake in 425° oven 55 to 60 minutes or until soft. Immediately cut slice from top of each. Carefully scoop out potato without breaking skin. Place potato in a large bowl. Add remaining ingredients and beat until smooth. Pile potato mixture into shells. Bake in 350° oven for 25 to 30 minutes. Makes 4 servings.

RAW POTATO DUMPLINGS

6 raw potatoes	Flour
2 eggs	Butter
Salt	

Peel and grate potatoes and let drain until most of the water is drawn off. Add the eggs and salt and beat well. Add enough flour to make a stiff dough. Knead and shape into dumplings. Drop into boiling salted water and cook gently. When dumplings come to the top, remove them, brush with butter and brown in the oven, or cut in half and brush with melted butter.

COTTAGE FRIED POTATOES

- 3 T. butter
- 3 c. cubed potatoes, cooked with skins on
- ¼ c. chopped onion
- ½ t. salt
- ⅛ t. pepper

Heat butter in large cast-iron skillet. Sauté onions until tender and transparent. Add cooled, peeled and cubed potatoes. Fry until golden brown on one side; carefully turn and brown on second side. Season with salt and pepper. Makes 4 to 6 servings.

SCALLOPED POTATOES

4 large potatoes	1½ t. salt
3 T. butter	⅛ t. pepper
⅓ c. chopped onion	2 c. milk
4½ t. flour	

Pare potatoes and cut into ⅛-inch crosswise slices. Place in a buttered 1½-quart baking dish. In a medium saucepan melt butter; add onion and cook until tender. Remove from heat and blend in flour, salt and pepper. Stir in milk. Return to heat and cook, stirring constantly, until mixture thickens slightly and comes to a boil. Pour over potato slices. Bake, covered, in a 350° oven for 30 minutes. Uncover and bake 1 hour longer, or until potatoes are tender. Makes 4 to 6 servings.

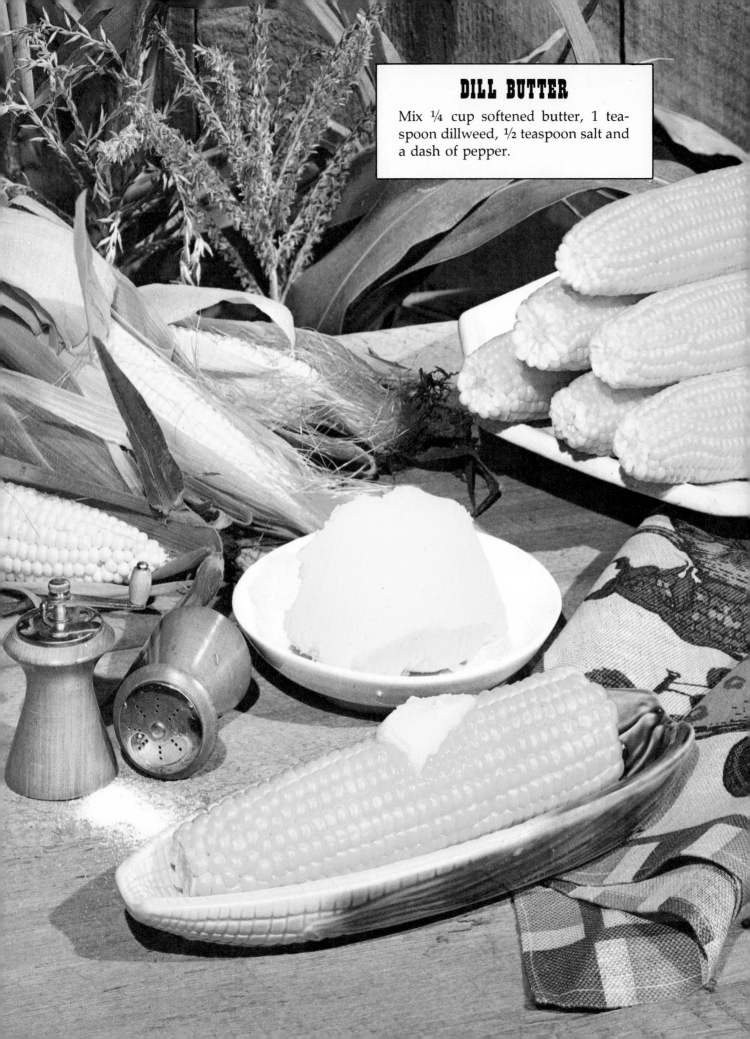

DILL BUTTER

Mix ¼ cup softened butter, 1 teaspoon dillweed, ½ teaspoon salt and a dash of pepper.

GLAZED BABY CARROTS

2 bunches baby carrots
6 T. butter
6 T. sugar
½ t. cinnamon or ginger

Wash carrots, scrape if necessary and leave whole. Cook in a small amount of boiling, salted water for 12 to 15 minutes or until tender when tested with a fork. Drain thoroughly. Combine butter, sugar and cinnamon or ginger in a large skillet. Cook, stirring constantly, until well blended. Add carrots and cook over low heat, shaking the pan frequently to glaze carrots on all sides until shiny and well glazed. Serves 6.

VINEGAR CARROTS

Wash and scrape 12 medium carrots. Boil until tender. Cut lengthwise in quarters and place in heated shallow serving dish. Season with salt, pepper, paprika and 2 tablespoons melted butter. Pour ⅓ cup hot cider vinegar over carrots. Serves 6 to 8.

CARROT-CELERY COMBO

1 bouillon cube
2¼ c. water, divided
½ t. salt
2 c. celery, sliced
2 c. carrots, sliced
2 T. cornstarch
Dash of Worcestershire, if desired

In a skillet dissolve bouillon cube in ¾ cup water, add salt, celery and carrots. Cook covered 8 to 10 minutes until tender. Moisten cornstarch with remaining 1½ cups water and thicken sauce slightly. Add dash of Worcestershire. Serves 6 to 8.

BAKED SQUASH

Wash 2 squash and cut them in half. Spoon out seeds and fibers from the cavity. Put 4 slices of bacon in a shallow baking pan and bake in a preheated 350° oven until crisp. Remove from oven, drain on paper towels and set aside. Sprinkle squash with salt and pepper and place, cut side down, in the bacon fat. Bake at 350° for about 1 hour or until tender when tested with a fork. Just before serving, sprinkle lightly with brown sugar, brush with some of the bacon fat, and drop the bacon, crumbled, into squash cavities. Serves 4.

GLAZED WINTER SQUASH

½ medium   ¼ c. brown sugar
  Hubbard squash   1 t. salt
⅓ c. butter   2 T. lemon juice

Cut squash in 1-inch cubes and peel. Melt butter; add brown sugar, salt and lemon juice. Pour over cubes of squash in a greased shallow baking pan. Cover and bake in a 400° oven about 45 minutes or until tender. Remove cover after 30 minutes of baking. Baste occasionally. Makes 4 to 6 servings.

TANGY STUFFED SQUASH

4 acorn squash
1 lb. chopped beef
¼ c. chopped onion
¼ c. bread crumbs
1½ t. salt
¼ t. dried tarragon
⅔ c. sour cream
½ t. hot pepper sauce

Cut squash in half. Scoop out seeds and fibers. Drop halves into boiling, salted water and cook about 10 minutes. Blend remaining ingredients. Mound meat filling into squash halves. Place halves in pan with 1 inch of hot water. Bake in a 350° oven for about 30 minutes or until squash is tender. Makes 4 to 6 servings.

Two generations ago, everyone raised rutabagas. Large piles of them were stored in cool, dark basements each fall, right alongside potatoes, cabbages, squash and pumpkins. Country cooks prepared them at least once a week and never failed to include at least part of one in their vegetable soup.

The rutabaga, a cross between a cabbage and a turnip, is a member of the mustard family. Its name comes from the Swedish word "Rotabagge." Most Europeans recognized the Swedish ability to prepare appealing "rutabagges" and in some areas rutabagas are called "Swedes" or "Swede turnips."

RUTABAGA-POTATO CASSEROLE

2 medium potatoes
2 medium rutabagas
½ c. flour
1 t. baking powder
1 t. salt
⅛ t. pepper, or to taste
4 eggs, well beaten
¼ c. milk
¼ c. melted butter

Peel potatoes and rutabagas; cover with cold water and let stand. Sift together flour, baking powder and seasonings. Blend half of dry ingredients with eggs, stir in milk and butter and mix well. Drain vegetables; run through blender or food grater. With a wooden spoon, mix remaining dry ingredients with vegetables. Work quickly so potatoes do not darken. Place mixture in greased 1-quart casserole. Set in pan of hot water with level at least ⅔ of the height of the casserole. Bake at 325° for one hour. Makes 6 servings.

RUTABAGA-ONION CASSEROLE

2 lbs. rutabaga, peeled and cut into
    ½-inch slices
3 c. thinly sliced onion
    Salt and pepper to taste
1 chicken bouillon cube
½ c. boiling water
2 T. butter

Arrange alternate layers of rutabaga and onions in a greased 2-quart casserole. Sprinkle layers lightly with salt and pepper. Dissolve bouillon in boiling water and pour over vegetables. Dot with butter. Cover and bake at 400° for 1¼ hours or until rutabagas are tender. Makes 6 servings.

RUTABAGAS IN SOUR CREAM

4 c. cubed rutabaga
¼ t. salt
    Dash pepper
1 medium onion,
    sliced
2 T. butter
1 c. sour cream
½ t. caraway or
    dill seed

Cook rutabaga in small amount of boiling salted water until tender, 15 - 20 minutes. Drain well. Sprinkle with salt and pepper. Sauté onion in butter until tender; add to sour cream. Pour over cubed rutabaga. Sprinkle with caraway or dill.

FRENCH FRIED RUTABAGAS

1 medium rutabaga
1 t. sugar
1 egg, beaten
½ c. cornmeal
1 t. salt
Vegetable oil
    for frying

Cut rutabaga slices lengthwise into ¼-inch strips. If the strips are too long, cut crosswise once. Parboil strips for 5 minutes in a small amount of boiling water with 1 teaspoon sugar added. Drain well and cool. Beat egg slightly in shallow bowl; mix cornmeal and salt together on waxed paper. Preheat frying pan to 370°. Add ¼ inch of oil. Dip cooled rutabaga strips in egg and roll in seasoned cornmeal. Without crowding, fry strips to brown evenly. Remove strips from skillet and place on baking sheets lined with paper towels. Keep warm in 250° oven while the remaining strips are cooked. Serve hot. Makes 4 to 6 servings.

MASHED RUTABAGAS AND POTATOES

4 c. (2 lbs.) sliced, pared rutabagas
3 c. quartered, pared potatoes (3 medium)
2 t. salt
1 T. sugar
1 chicken bouillon cube
2 c. boiling water
¼ t. pepper
1 c. grated cheddar cheese
2 T. finely chopped onion

Place rutabagas, potatoes, salt and sugar in saucepan. Dissolve bouillon cube in boiling water and pour over vegetables. Quickly bring to a boil, reduce heat and continue cooking gently until vegetables are tender. Drain, mash and add pepper, grated cheese and onion. Beat until fluffy. Top with buttered crumbs and broil until golden brown if desired. Makes 6 servings.

Sauerkraut was probably the first food to travel around the world. It has come a long way since the days when chunks of wine-fermented cabbage were fed to hardworking Chinese coolies building the Great Wall of China.

German and Dutch settlers brought their kraut-making skills with them to the new colonies. Cabbage grew well in the New World.

In autumn, you could count on a trip to Grandmother's cellar to sample the tawny kraut working mysteriously in the big crock. Grandmother's tangy kraut had a wide variety of uses, from stuffing pork or poultry to baking a cake.

BEEF WITH SAUERKRAUT

2 T. vegetable oil
3 lbs. eye round or chuck beef,
   cut into 2-inch cubes
1½ c. sliced onions
1½ t. salt
 ½ t. freshly ground black pepper
 1 t. paprika
1½ lbs. sauerkraut, rinsed and drained
 1 bay leaf
1½ c. chopped canned tomatoes

Heat the oil in a casserole; brown the meat and onions. Sprinkle with salt, pepper and paprika. Cover and cook over low heat for 20 minutes; watch carefully and add a little water if necessary to keep from burning. Mix in the sauerkraut. Cook 10 minutes. Add the bay leaf and tomatoes. Cover and cook 1½ hours longer. Discard bay leaf. Serves 6 to 8.

BAKED SAUERKRAUT

 ½ c. chopped onion
 ½ c. green pepper strips
 2 T. shortening
10 pineapple slices with liquid
 2 T. cornstarch
 1 c. beef bouillon
 1 t. soy sauce
 2 t. vinegar
 ¼ c. sugar
 ⅛ t. pepper
 ½ t. ground ginger
 4 c. sauerkraut, drained
 9 hot dogs, cut in half

Sauté onion and green pepper in shortening until tender. Drain pineapple, reserving liquid; mix half the pineapple liquid with cornstarch and add to onion and green pepper. Gradually blend in remaining pineapple liquid and bouillon. Stir in soy sauce, vinegar, sugar, pepper and ginger. Cook until thickened. Arrange half the sauerkraut and half the pineapple slices in the bottom of a 3½-quart casserole. Top with half the sauce mixture. Add remaining sauerkraut and pineapple. Pile hot dogs in center and pour remaining sauce over all. Bake at 350° for 30 minutes. Makes 6 to 8 servings.

SAUERKRAUT RELISH

3 c. sauerkraut, well drained
   and chopped
1 c. chopped onion
2 c. chopped celery
1 large green pepper, chopped
1½ c. sugar
1½ c. water
 ½ c. vinegar

Combine sauerkraut, onion, celery and green pepper. Set aside. In a medium saucepan, combine sugar, water and vinegar. Bring liquid mixture to a boil to dissolve sugar. Cool. Add liquid mixture to vegetable mixture and mix well. Let stand in refrigerator for 24 hours. Makes 6 to 8 servings.

CRISPY KRAUT SALAD

2 c. finely chopped sauerkraut
 ½ c. chopped onion
 ½ c. chopped celery
 ¼ c. chopped green pepper
 1 c. chopped pimiento
 ½ c. cider vinegar
 ¼ c. salad oil
 ½ c. sugar

Drain kraut well. Chop onion, celery, green pepper and pimiento. Make a dressing from vinegar, oil and sugar. Blend all ingredients together and marinate for an hour or longer. Makes 6 servings.

SCALLOPED SAUERKRAUT AND TOMATOES

2½ c. whole stewed tomatoes
   Salt
   Pepper
 2 T. butter
 2 c. bread crumbs
2½ c. sauerkraut

Drain tomatoes, reserving liquid. Put tomato pieces in greased baking dish. Sprinkle with salt and pepper. Dot with butter. Cover with layer of crumbs. Add layer of sauerkraut. Alternate layers, seasoning and dotting each with butter, until all ingredients are used. Have layer of buttered crumbs on top. Add tomato liquid. Bake at 400° 20 minutes. Serves 6.

SALADS

WILTED LETTUCE TOSS

4 slices bacon
¼ c. sliced green onion
1 large tomato, chopped
4 c. torn leaf lettuce
2 T. vinegar
¼ t. salt
    Dash pepper

Fry bacon in large skillet until crisp; drain, reserving 1 tablespoon drippings. Crumble bacon and set aside. Meanwhile, combine lettuce, tomato and onion. In skillet, heat reserved drippings, vinegar, salt and pepper to boiling. Gradually add lettuce mixture, tossing only until leaves are coated and wilted slightly. Turn into serving bowl. Top with crumbled bacon. Serve immediately. Makes 4 to 5 servings.

CREAMY CELERY SLAW

1 t. salt	¼ c. sour cream
1½ t. sugar	2 c. celery, thinly
⅛ t. pepper	sliced on diagonal
Dash paprika	1 pimiento, slivered
⅓ c. salad oil	2 T. wine vinegar

Combine salt, sugar, pepper, paprika, oil and vinegar; beat well with hand beater; then slowly beat in sour cream. Pour this dressing over celery. Marinate in refrigerator about 3 hours; then toss in pimiento. Makes 3 servings.

TOMATO FRENCH DRESSING

1 c. tomato juice	1 t. paprika
½ c. corn oil	1 t. salt
¼ c. vinegar	1 t. Worcestershire
2 T. sugar	sauce
1 t. dry mustard	1 clove garlic

Measure all ingredients into a bottle or jar. Cover tightly and shake well. Chill several hours, then remove garlic. Shake thoroughly before serving. Makes about 2 cups.

ORANGE SLAW

3 medium or 4 small oranges
1 small head cabbage
¼ small onion
¾ c. mayonnaise
1 T. fresh squeezed lemon juice
1 T. sugar
½ t. salt

Peel oranges and cut into bite-sized pieces. Shred cabbage using long blade of grater, or cut finely with sharp knife. Chop onion finely. Place oranges, cabbage and onion in large serving bowl. Mix together mayonnaise, lemon juice, sugar and salt. Pour over slaw and mix lightly. Cover and refrigerate for 20 to 30 minutes before serving. Makes 6 servings.

TUNA - BEAN SALAD

1 c. chunk light tuna, drained
¾ c. celery, chopped
¼ c. onion, chopped
¼ c. sweet pickle relish
¾ t. curry powder
½ c. mayonnaise
2 hard-cooked eggs, chopped
¼ t. salt
1 15-oz. can red kidney beans, drained and rinsed
¼ c. chopped nuts

Lightly mix all ingredients, except nuts. Line serving bowl with salad greens and fill with mixture. Top with chopped nuts. Makes 4 to 6 servings.

CREAMY COTTAGE - POTATO SALAD

Add 2 cups (16 ounces) creamed cottage cheese to each 3 cups of your favorite cold potato salad. Chill well. Makes 6 to 8 servings.

They called them the "meetin' seeds." Colonists grew fennel, dill and caraway seeds in their gardens and carried them to church to nibble during long Sabbath sermons.

From pickles to salads, delightful seeds accent country kitchen fare. Dill, perhaps the most familiar today, was also used medicinally and as a nerve-calming tea in medieval times. Some claim its name is derived from the Norse word "dilla," meaning to lull. The Greeks, however, reportedly chewed on dill seeds to keep them awake. Some cultures prescribed the seeds as a cure for insomnia. Others used it to hinder a witch's will.

The European native, with a parasol of yellow-green flowers on tall, flowing stems, is at home in backyard gardens. Country cooks have always prized dill seeds for their tasty pickle flavoring. Other country kitchen treats can be flavored by dropping a pinch or two in a green apple pie or scattering some across a summer salad.

DEVIL-DILLED EGGS

8 hard-boiled eggs
¼ c. mayonnaise
¼ t. chopped dillweed
Dash of pepper
Paprika (optional)

Cut eggs into halves. Remove yolks, mash and mix with remaining ingredients except paprika. Spoon yolk mixture into whites. Garnish with paprika, if desired. Chill before serving.

DILLY DRESSING

1 c. tomato juice
1 t. grated lemon rind
2 T. fresh lemon juice or wine vinegar
1 t. salt
½ t. fresh or dried dillweed
½ t. dry mustard
¼ t. liquid sugar substitute

Combine all ingredients in a jar. Shake to blend. Chill. Serve with tossed salad or over sliced tomatoes with onion rings. Makes about 1 cup.

CREAMY CELERY SEED DRESSING

½ c. dairy
    sour cream
2 T. milk
1 t. chopped chives
¾ t. celery seed
¼ t. salt
¼ t. pepper
1 T. vinegar

In a small bowl combine sour cream, milk, chives, celery seed, salt and pepper. Mix well. Blend in vinegar. Serve with molded vegetable salads, cucumbers, tomatoes, tossed salads, etc. Makes about ½ cup.

HERB DRESSING

¾ c. mayonnaise
1 hard-boiled egg, finely chopped
2 T. finely chopped parsley
1½ t. tarragon vinegar
½ t. prepared mustard
1 t. finely chopped chives

Blend all ingredients. Chill. Serve with mixed greens, vegetables or meat salads. Makes one cup.

COTTAGE CHEESE DRESSING

½ cup French dressing
½ cup mayonnaise
½ cup cottage cheese

Fold French dressing into mayonnaise. Lightly fold in cottage cheese. Chill. Serve with fruit, vegetable or mixed green salads. Makes 1¼ cups.

FRUIT SALAD DRESSING

½ c. mayonnaise
½ c. dairy sour cream
2½ T. confectioners' sugar
1½ T. lemon juice

Blend all ingredients. Chill about one hour. Serve with fruit salads. Makes about 1¼ cups.

FRUITS

As any country cook can tell you, happiness is a strawberry patch filled with plump, juicy, red berries. Strawberries, plain, with cream and sugar, or in a classical shortcake, are natural country kitchen treats.

No one really knows how strawberries picked up their name. Perhaps some distant country gardener first referred to them as strawberries when she covered them with mulch. Another theory speculates that the specks on the berry resemble straw.

The Indians showed the colonists how to bruise the wild strawberries in a mortar, mix them with meal and make a strawberry bread. They also taught colonists how to sweeten the berries with the dew of milkweed.

Every country cook has her favorite strawberry recipes to please her family. Strawberry shortcake probably tops the list. Have you ever tried fresh crushed and sweetened berries over your favorite rice custard? Delicious.

STRAWBERRY SURPRISE

½ c. milk
1½ c. miniature marshmallows
1 c. whipping cream
½ c. sliced almonds
2½ c. fresh strawberries, cut in half

Heat milk to boiling, add marshmallows and stir at medium heat until marshmallows melt. Remove from heat and allow to cool thoroughly. Whip cream; fold berries and whipped cream into cooled marshmallow mixture. Pour into sherbet dishes and chill several hours. When ready to serve, sprinkle sliced almonds on top or garnish with fresh mint leaves. Serves 6.

STRAWBERRY-RHUBARB COBBLER

2 qts. drained stemmed fresh strawberries
2 qts. drained ½-inch pieces fresh rhubarb (about 2½ lbs.)
5 c. (2¼ lbs.) sugar
¾ c. quick-cooking tapioca
1 t. salt
1 T. butter
Unbaked biscuits (your favorite recipe)

To prepare and freeze filling: Combine fruits, sugar, tapioca and salt; mix well. Divide filling mixture evenly among four 1-quart aluminum foil baking pans, taking care that filling is at least ¾-inch below top of pans. Cover with aluminum foil, sealing close to surface of fruits. Freeze firmly. Filling may be stored in freezer up to six months.

To bake each cobbler: Bake covered pan of frozen filling at 425° for 50 minutes or until filling is bubbling. Then remove cover, dot filling with butter, and top with 8 unbaked biscuits. Return to oven and bake 20 minutes longer, covering biscuits loosely with aluminum foil during last 5 minutes to prevent overbrowning. Serve warm. Each cobbler makes 8 servings. Makes 4 cobblers.

STRAWBERRY SHORTCAKE

2 c. flour
4 t. baking powder
½ t. salt
1 T. sugar
⅓ c. shortening
¾ c. milk
Butter
Whipping cream
Whole strawberries

GARNISH
2 qts. fresh strawberries, mashed and sweetened to taste

Preheat oven to 450°. Sift flour, baking powder, salt and sugar together and cut in shortening. Gradually stir in milk to make a soft dough. On a floured board, knead dough 8 to 10 times, then roll to ½-inch thickness. Cut with large cookie cutter and place on greased cookie sheet or bake as one sheet on greased cookie sheet and cut into squares after baking. Bake 12 to 15 minutes. Remove shortcake from oven, split and butter immediately. Keep warm until ready to serve (wrap in foil) or serve immediately. Place warm shortcake (bottom halves) in individual bowls. Spoon strawberries over shortcake halves, place remaining half on top and spoon more berries on top. Garnish with whipping cream and whole strawberries. Serves 6 to 8.

RHUBARB-CUSTARD KUCHEN

CRUST

½ c. butter	½ c. sugar
1 egg yolk	1¼ c. flour
½ t. salt	¼ c. water
2½ c. rhubarb	½ t. nutmeg

CUSTARD

2 eggs	¼ t. salt
1 egg white	¼ c. milk
¾ c. sugar	1 t. vanilla

Cream butter, sugar, salt and egg yolk together well. Then add flour. Moisten like pie crust, using milk. Pat into 10 x 12-inch pan. Bring rhubarb and water to boil in small pan, cooking only until rhubarb begins to soften. Cool slightly. Pour rhubarb into lined pan. Beat together eggs, egg white, sugar, salt, milk and vanilla. Pour over rhubarb. Sprinkle nutmeg over all. Bake at 350° for 45 minutes. Serve warm or cooled in 2½-inch squares topped with whipped cream.

RHUBARB CREAM PIE

1½ c. sugar	2 eggs, well-beaten
3 T. flour	3 c. cut rhubarb
1 t. nutmeg	Pastry for
1½ T. butter	double-crust pie

Blend sugar, flour, nutmeg and butter. Add eggs; beat until smooth; pour over rhubarb in 9-inch pastry-lined pie pan. Top with pastry. Bake at 450° for 10 minutes, then at 350° about 30 minutes. Serve warm or cooled.

RHUBARB BETTY

5 c. rhubarb, cut in ½-inch pieces
1¾ c. sugar
1 T. flour
½ t. salt
2 t. grated orange rind
1 orange, sectioned and cubed
4 c. small bread cubes
½ c. butter, melted
½ c. flaked coconut

Mix together rhubarb, sugar, flour, salt, 1 teaspoon of the orange rind and fruit. Add half of bread cubes and half of butter; mix. Put into greased 8 x 8 x 2-inch baking pan. Combine remaining bread cubes, butter, orange rind and coconut. Sprinkle over top of rhubarb. Bake at 375° for about 40 minutes or until browned. Serve warm. Makes 6 to 8 servings.

RHUBARB COBBLER

1 c. sugar	1½ t. baking
2 T. cornstarch	powder
½ t. cinnamon	½ t. salt
4 c. rhubarb, cut	4 T. butter
in 1-inch pieces	⅓ c. milk
1 T. water	½ c. chopped
2 T. butter	pecans
1 c. flour	1 t. shredded
⅓ c. sugar	orange peel

Combine the 1 cup sugar, cornstarch and cinnamon. Add rhubarb and water. Cook and stir until mixture is boiling; cook 1 minute longer. Pour into 8 x 1½-inch round baking dish; dot with the 2 tablespoons butter. Place in 400° oven while preparing biscuits. Sift together flour, ⅓ cup sugar, baking powder and salt. Cut in 4 tablespoons butter. Stir in milk, pecans and orange peel. Drop spoonfuls of butter onto hot rhubarb mixture. Bake in 400° oven for about 25 minutes. Serve with light cream or milk. Makes 6 servings.

Cherries play a vital part in our nation's heritage. Every American student knows the legend of George Washington cutting down his father's cherry tree. Washington's birthday has become the traditional time to offer cherry desserts in country kitchens.

We can thank Queen Bess of England for giving us the cherry pie. She received some preserved cherries for a gift and she liked them so well she ordered a 30 acre cherry orchard planted on the royal grounds. When the trees matured, Elizabeth ordered the cherries baked into pies. Thus did cherry pies appear on the menus for English royal banquets.

CHERRY CHIFFON PIE

2 c. frozen cherries, thawed
5 T. sugar
½ c. water
1 T. lemon juice
1 pkg. cherry flavored gelatin
¼ t. almond extract
1 c. evaporated milk, chilled
1 baked 9-inch pie shell

Drain cherries, saving juice. Cut cherries in half; combine with juice, sugar, water and lemon juice. Cook over low heat for 4 or 5 minutes. Pour mixture over gelatin, stir until dissolved and add almond extract; chill until slightly thickened. Whip evaporated milk until stiff peaks form; fold into cherry mixture and chill for 10 minutes. Pile lightly into baked pie shell. Chill at least 3 hours before serving. Makes 1 pie.

CHERRY SAUCE I

2½ c. canned, pitted, sour red cherries
2 T. lemon juice
1 T. cornstarch
¾ c. sugar
½ t. almond extract
1 qt. ice cream

Drain cherries, reserving one cup juice. Place cherries, lemon juice and reserved cherry juice in a saucepan. Combine cornstarch and sugar; add to cherry mixture. Cook over medium heat, stirring constantly until thickened and mixture comes to a boil. Cook slightly; stir in almond extract. Serve warm or cold over cherry or vanilla ice cream. Makes about 2¾ cups sauce, or 6 to 8 servings.

OLD-FASHIONED CHERRY PIE

2½ T. tapioca
⅛ t. salt
1 c. sugar
3 c. drained tart cherries
½ c. cherry juice
¼ t. almond extract
1 T. butter
9-inch pie shell

Mix together all ingredients except butter and let stand 15 minutes. Pour into pie shell; dot with butter. Add top crust. Bake at 425° for about 45 minutes. Makes 6 to 8 servings.

CHERRY SPONGE PUDDING

2 T. quick-cooking tapioca
½ c. sugar
⅛ t. salt
2½ c. sour cherries and juice
1 T. lemon juice
1 T. butter
½ c. sifted flour
2 eggs, unbeaten
¼ t. cream of tartar
⅛ t. salt
½ c. sugar

Combine tapioca, sugar, salt, cherries and juice in saucepan. Cook and stir over medium heat until mixture comes to a boil. Add lemon juice and butter; blend. Remove from heat. If desired, add a few drops of red coloring. Pour into a 2-quart baking dish and keep warm. Measure sifted flour and set aside. Combine eggs, cream of tartar and salt in bowl. Beat with eggbeater until foamy. Then add sugar gradually and continue beating until very fluffy, thick and light-colored. Gradually fold in flour. Pour the batter over warm fruit. Bake in 325° oven for 50 minutes or until cake is baked. Serve warm. Makes 8 servings.

CHERRY SAUCE II

2½ c. tart red cherries
1 c. cherry juice
4 t. cornstarch
¼ c. sugar

In a 2-quart saucepan, combine cornstarch and sugar. Gradually stir in cherry juice. Cook, stirring constantly, till thick and clear. Add cherries. Heat through. Makes 2 cups.

DESSERTS

OLD-FASHIONED RICE PUDDING

2 large eggs	½ c. seedless raisins
½ c. sugar	½ c. chopped
½ t. salt	cooking apples
2 c. milk	1 t. vanilla
2 c. cooked rice	Dash nutmeg

Blend together eggs, sugar and salt. Scald milk. Slowly stir into egg mixture. Blend. Add rice, raisins, apples and vanilla. Mix well. Pour into a 3-quart casserole. Sprinkle top with nutmeg. Set casserole in a pan of water and bake in a 350° oven for 1 hour and 15 minutes. Bake until knife inserted into pudding comes out clean. Serve warm with cream or milk. Makes 6 servings.

BLUEBERRY TREASURE SQUARES

2 c. crisp rice cereal
½ c. chopped almonds, toasted
½ c. flaked coconut, toasted
½ c. brown sugar
⅓ c. butter, melted
1 qt. vanilla ice cream
½ c. blueberry ice-cream topping

Mix rice cereal which has been slightly crushed with almonds, coconut, brown sugar and butter. Press ½ of mixture in bottom of 9 x 9 x 2-inch pan. Chill. Stir vanilla ice cream to soften. Add topping and quickly swirl through ice cream to marble. Freeze. Makes 9 servings. Serve with topping, if desired.

FRESH BLUEBERRY TOPPING

Combine ¼ cup sugar, 2 teaspoons cornstarch, dash each salt, cinnamon and cloves. Stir in 2 cups fresh blueberries (slightly crushed) and ⅓ cup light corn syrup. Cook and stir till mixture boils; simmer 7 minutes. Cool; add 2 tablespoons lemon juice. Makes 1½ cups.

HONEY-GLAZED FRUITS

4 c. canned pear halves, drained
2 c. canned sliced pineapple, drained
⅓ c. honey
½ t. grated fresh orange rind
8 maraschino cherries with stems, drained

In shallow baking pan, place 1 pear half on top of each of 8 pineapple slices. Stir together honey and orange rind. Spoon over fruits. Broil 4 to 6 inches from heat until thoroughly heated, 3 to 4 minutes. Garnish with cherries. Makes 8 servings.

Hidden in the memories of long-past summer days, there is a hand-cranked ice-cream freezer on the back porch of our childhood home.

Ice cream became a socially acceptable dessert when Dolly Madison created a sensation at her husband's second inaugural ball serving "high on a silver platter a large shining dome of pink ice cream."

However, it wasn't until Nancy Johnson invented the hand-cranked ice-cream freezer in 1846 that homemade ice cream became common in country kitchens. Nancy, by the way, forgot to patent her machine, so William Young, who did, received all the credit.

VANILLA ICE CREAM (Custard Base)

1½ c. sugar
¼ c. flour
Dash salt
2 c. milk
4 eggs, slightly beaten
1 qt. (4 cups) heavy cream
1 T. vanilla

Combine sugar, flour and salt in a large saucepan; stir in milk. Cook over medium heat, stirring constantly, until mixture thickens and bubbles 1 minute. Stir half the hot mixture slowly into beaten eggs in a medium-size bowl; stir back into remaining mixture in saucepan. Cook, stirring, for 1 minute. Pour into a large bowl; stir in cream and vanilla. Chill at least 2 hours. Pour mixture into a 4- to 6-quart freezer can; freeze following directions of your freezer. Pack in plastic containers; freeze until firm. Makes about 2 quarts.

PUMPKIN CHIFFON PIE

    2 envelopes unflavored gelatin
 ¼ c. cold water
    2 eggs, separated
 1½ c. canned pumpkin
    1 c. milk
 ¾ c. brown sugar, firmly packed
    2 t. pumpkin pie spice
 ½ t. salt
 ½ pt. (1 cup) whipping cream, whipped
    9-inch graham cracker crumb crust

Soften gelatin in cold water. Beat egg yolks. Add pumpkin, milk, one-half cup brown sugar, spice and salt to yolks. Cook over low heat, stirring constantly, until thickened. Add gelatin; stir to dissolve. Chill until mixture thickens. Beat egg whites until they hold soft peaks. Add remaining one-fourth cup brown sugar and continue beating until egg whites are stiff. Fold into pumpkin mixture, then fold in whipped cream. Pour into crust. Chill until firm. Makes one 9-inch pie.

PUMPKIN-APPLE TARTS

    2 c. canned pumpkin
    2 c. applesauce
    1 c. light brown sugar
 1½ t. salt
    3 t. cinnamon
    2 t. nutmeg
 ½ t. ginger
    1 t. cloves
    8 eggs, beaten
    1 c. heavy cream
 ½ c. milk
   10 5-inch unbaked pastry shells

Combine pumpkin, applesauce, sugar, salt and spices. Add eggs. Scald cream and milk; add slowly to pumpkin mixture, mixing well. Pour into individual pastry shells. Bake in 400° oven for 40 minutes or until knife inserted near center of pie comes out clean. Cool. Garnish with whipped cream, candy shot, cheese wedges or walnut halves. Makes 10 servings.

PUMPKIN CAKE

 2¼ c. flour
    3 t. baking powder
 ½ t. salt
 ¼ t. baking soda
 1½ t. cinnamon
 ½ t. ginger
 ½ t. allspice
 ½ c. butter
    1 c. brown sugar, firmly packed
 ½ c. granulated sugar
    2 eggs, unbeaten
 ¾ c. buttermilk or sour milk
 ¾ c. canned pumpkin
 ½ c. chopped nuts

Measure flour and add baking powder, salt, soda and spices. Mix together. Cream butter and add sugars gradually. Cream well. Add eggs, one at a time, beating until light. Add flour mixture alternately with buttermilk in small amounts. After each addition beat until smooth. Add pumpkin and nuts. Mix well. Bake in greased 9 x 13-inch pan in a 350° oven for 30 minutes or until done. Frost with a plain butter frosting.

PUMPKIN PIE

    2 eggs, slightly beaten
 ½ c. brown sugar
 ½ c. granulated sugar
    2 c. pumpkin
    2 c. top milk
    1 T. flour
 ½ t. ginger
 ½ t. salt
 1½ t. cinnamon
 ½ t. nutmeg
    Pastry for one-crust, 10-inch pie

Beat eggs and sugars; add pumpkin and milk. Add flour mixed with salt and spices. Beat well. Pour into 10-inch pastry-lined pie pan. Bake in 450° oven 10 minutes; reduce heat to 325° and bake 40 minutes longer, or until a knife inserted near center of pie comes out clean.

TOMATO SOUP CAKE

2 c. flour
1⅓ c. sugar
4 t. baking powder
1 t. baking soda
1½ t. allspice
1 t. cinnamon
½ t. ground cloves
1 10¾-oz. can condensed tomato soup
½ c. vegetable shortening
2 eggs
¼ c. water
1 c. raisins or chopped nuts

Measure dry ingredients into large bowl. Add soup and shortening. Beat for two minutes, scraping sides and bottom of bowl constantly. Add eggs and water. Beat two minutes more, scraping bowl frequently. Add raisins or nuts. Pour into either two round layers or a 13 x 9 x 2-inch pan that has been generously greased and floured. Bake at 350° for 35 to 40 minutes. Let stand in pans 10 minutes, remove and cool on rack. Frost with your favorite icing.

CARROT CAKE

½ c. shortening	2 c. flour
1 c. brown sugar	¼ t. baking soda
½ c. granulated sugar	3 t. baking powder
	1 t. salt
1 egg	1 t. cinnamon
¾ c. cooked, mashed carrots	⅔ c. chopped nuts
	⅓ c. sour milk

Cream shortening and sugars together. Add egg and mashed carrots. Sift flour, soda, baking powder, salt and cinnamon together. Add nuts and dry ingredients alternately with sour milk. Mix batter well. Pour into two 8-inch square pans with greased and floured paper in the bottoms. Bake 25 minutes at 350°. Cool. Put layers together with your favorite butter icing or whipped cream.

HOMEMADE MINCEMEAT

½ lb. fresh beef suet, chopped fine
4 c. seedless raisins
2 c. dried currants
1¼ c. chopped candied fruit
½ c. chopped dried figs
4 c. chopped, peeled cored apples
1 c. coarsely chopped nuts
1¼ c. sugar
1 t. ground nutmeg
1 t. ground allspice
1 t. ground cinnamon
½ t. ground cloves
2½ c. brandy
1 c. dry red wine

Combine the suet, fruit, nuts, sugar and spices in a large mixing bowl and stir together thoroughly. Pour in the brandy and wine, and mix with a large wooden spoon until all ingredients are well-moistened. Cover the bowl and set the mincemeat aside in a cool place (not in the refrigerator) for at least three weeks.

Check the mincemeat once a week. As the liquid is absorbed by the fruit, replenish it with wine and brandy, using about ¼ cup of each at a time. Mincemeat can be kept indefinitely in a covered container in the refrigerator. Makes 3 quarts.

To make pies with homemade mincemeat, prepare your favorite pastry for a two-crust pie. Line the pan with the bottom crust. Add undrained mincemeat. Add top crust. Bake in 425° oven 30 minutes or until done.

OLD-FASHIONED MINCEMEAT PIE

3 c. prepared mincemeat
1½ c. coarsely broken walnuts
½ c. brown sugar, packed
½ c. brandy
Pastry for two-crust pie
4 T. butter, softened
1 T. light cream
Pastry for two-crust, 9-inch pie

Combine walnuts, mincemeat, brown sugar and brandy; refrigerate to allow flavors to mingle. You can do this for several days. Roll out pastry for bottom crust, spread with two tablespoons butter; fold into thirds; refrigerate until well chilled; repeat with top crust. Heat oven to 425°. Roll out pastry crust. Fill with undrained mincemeat mixture. Adjust top crust; brush top with light cream. Bake 30 minutes or until nicely browned.

CHERRY PIE

Pastry for one-crust, 9-inch pie
c. ground cherries, husked
2 eggs
¼ t. salt
¾ c. sugar
1⅓ T. flour
1 c. milk
1 t. vanilla

Line pie pan with pastry and fill with ground cherries. Beat eggs with salt and add sugar and flour. Add milk and vanilla and stir well. Pour over cherries and bake in 425° oven 10 minutes, then reduce temperature to 350° and bake 25 to 30 minutes longer or until a knife inserted in center comes out clean. Cover with whipped cream topping. Makes 1 9-inch pie.

SOUR CREAM RAISIN PIE

2 eggs, slightly beaten
¾ c. sugar
¼ t. salt
1 t. cinnamon
½ t. nutmeg
¼ t. cloves
1 c. sour cream
1 c. seeded raisins
Pastry for one-crust, 8-inch pie

Combine ingredients; pour into 8-inch pastry-lined pie pan. Bake in 450° oven 10 minutes, then in 350° oven about 30 minutes, or until mixture doesn't stick to knife. Serve warm or cold.

BLACKBERRY PIE

4 c. fresh blackberries
1 c. sugar
2 T. flour
2 T. lemon juice
¼ t. salt
Pastry for two-crust, 9-inch pie
1 T. butter

Combine berries, sugar, flour, lemon juice and salt. Line pie pan with pastry, add filling, dot with butter and cover with top crust. Bake in 450° oven 10 minutes; reduce temperature to 350° and bake 25 to 30 minutes longer. Makes 1 9-inch pie.

LEMON CREME PIE

1 c. sugar
¼ c. cornstarch
3 egg yolks, beaten
3 T. cold water
1¼ c. water
1 T. butter
6 T. lemon juice
1 T. grated lemon peel
1 9-inch baked pastry shell

Mix cornstarch with sugar. Beat egg yolks until lemon-colored. Add 3 tablespoons cold water. Stir into cornstarch-sugar mixture. Blend well. Bring 1¼ cups water to boil. Slowly add the above mixture to boiling water and cook until clear and thick, about 5 minutes. Add butter, lemon juice, and lemon peel. Return to heat and cook 2 additional minutes. Remove from heat. Cool. Pour into baked 9-inch pie shell.

MERINGUE

3 egg whites
4 T. confectioners' sugar

Beat egg whites until stiff but not dry; add sugar gradually; spread over cooled filling, sealing to edges of pastry. Brown in 350° oven 13 to 15 minutes.

GOLDEN APPLE-PECAN PIE

2 Golden Delicious apples, peeled and sliced
3 eggs
¾ c. brown sugar
⅛ t. salt
¾ c. light corn syrup
2 t. butter
⅔ c. coarsely chopped pecans
Pastry for single-crust pie

Line a 9-inch pie plate with pastry. Place apple slices in bottom of pie plate. Beat eggs; add remaining ingredients, reserving a few pecan halves or large pieces, and mix well. Bake at 425° for 10 minutes. Then reduce heat to 300° and bake for about one hour or until set. Garnish with whipped cream and a few pecan halves.

CAKES

KWIK KRAZY KAKE

1½ c. all-purpose flour
1 t. baking soda
½ t. salt
1 t. cinnamon
1 c. sugar
¼ c. cocoa
½ c. whole-bran cereal
1 c. cold strong coffee
¼ c. vegetable oil
1 T. vinegar
1 t. vanilla

Sift together flour, soda, salt, cinnamon, sugar and cocoa. Set aside. Measure whole bran cereal and coffee into ungreased 8 x 8 x 2-inch baking pan; stir to combine. Let stand 1 to 2 minutes or until most of liquid is absorbed. Mix in oil, vinegar and vanilla. Add sifted dry ingredients; stir until smooth. Bake in 350° oven about 40 minutes or until wooden pick inserted near center comes out clean. Serve with cinnamon-flavored whipped topping, orange or lemon sauce or ice cream. Sprinkle with nuts, if desired.

POOR MAN'S CAKE

1 c. light brown sugar, firmly packed
1 c. water
⅜ c. shortening
1 c. seeded raisins
1 t. cinnamon
½ t. nutmeg
½ t. salt
2¼ c. cake flour
1 t. baking soda
1¼ t. baking powder

Combine sugar, water, shortening, raisins, spices and salt in a medium saucepan. Bring to a boil over medium heat and boil for 3 minutes, stirring constantly. Cool. Measure sifted flour, add soda and baking powder and sift again. Gradually stir dry ingredients into raisin mixture. Then beat well. Pour into an 8 x 4 x 3-inch loaf pan, which has been greased generously on bottom and sides. Bake in a 325° oven for about one hour.

PRUNE SPICE CAKE

⅔ c. prune pulp
1½ c. flour
½ t. cinnamon
½ t. nutmeg
½ t. allspice
½ t. baking soda
¼ t. salt
½ c. butter
1½ c. sugar
2 eggs
⅔ c. buttermilk
½ c. chopped nuts

Chop unsweetened cooked prunes, measure correct amount and set aside. Sift together flour, spices, baking soda and salt. Set this aside, too. Cream butter until soft, then work in sugar, a little at a time, as thoroughly as possible. Add eggs and beat well, then stir in prune pulp. Stir in flour mixture and buttermilk alternately, beginning and ending with flour. Stir in nuts. Pour into a greased 10-inch tube pan and bake at 350° for 50 to 60 minutes or until cake pulls away from the sides of pan. Cool about 10 minutes before turning out of pan. Cool completely before covering with your favorite butter icing.

CHOCOLATE CHIP CAKE

1 c. dates, chopped fine
1 t. baking soda
1¼ c. boiling water
¾ c. shortening
1 c. sugar
2 eggs
1 t. baking powder
¾ t. salt
1½ c. flour

TOPPING:

½ c. brown sugar
1 c. chocolate chips
½ c. chopped nuts

Chop dates into fine pieces and sprinkle with baking soda. Pour boiling water over the mixture. Set aside. Cream shortening and sugar. Blend in eggs. Add baking powder, salt and flour. Mix well; add date mixture. Beat until well blended. Pour into greased 9 x 13 x 2-inch pan. Sprinkle topping mixture over cake batter. Bake in 350° oven for 40 minutes.

HARVEST SPICE CAKE

¾ c. butter, softened
1½ c. light brown sugar, firmly packed
3 eggs
3 c. flour
1 T. baking powder
2 t. baking soda
1½ t. salt
½ t. ground allspice
½ t. ground nutmeg
½ t. ground cinnamon
1 c. apple cider
¾ c. milk

Cream together butter and sugar. Beat in eggs, one at a time. Stir together dry ingredients. Combine cider and milk. Thoroughly blend flour into creamed mixture alternately with cider mixture, beginning and ending with flour. Pour into three greased, wax-paper-lined, 8-inch round cake pans or into greased and floured 9 x 13-inch cake pan. Bake in preheated 350° oven 25 to 30 minutes or until cake tests done. Cool 10 minutes before removing from pans. Cool completely before frosting with your favorite icing or BUTTER RUM FROSTING. Decorate with walnuts if desired.

RAISIN-APPLE SPICE CAKE

2½ c. flour
1½ t. soda
1 t. salt
1 t. cinnamon
½ t. cloves
½ t. nutmeg
¾ c. butter
1¼ c. sugar
2 eggs
½ c. light molasses
2¼ c. thick applesauce
½ c. finely chopped nuts
   Raisin Penuche Icing
   English walnut halves

Sift flour with soda, salt and spices. Cream butter, add sugar gradually and beat until fluffy. Add eggs one at a time. Add molasses and beat thoroughly. Stir in applesauce and nuts. Gradually blend in sifted dry ingredients. Pour batter into two wax-paper-lined and greased 8- or 9-inch square baking pans, or three 8-inch round layer pans. Bake in a 350° oven for 20 to 25 minutes. Spread cooled layers with Raisin Penuche Icing and stack. Frost sides. Garnish with English walnut halves.

BUTTER RUM FROSTING

1 c. butter, softened
4 c. confectioners' sugar
⅓ c. dark corn syrup
2 t. rum extract

Cream butter. Add sugar and syrup alternately to butter, beating well after each addition. Beat in rum extract. If necessary add more sugar until proper spreading consistency is reached.

RAISIN PENUCHE ICING

⅓ c. butter
⅓ c. brown sugar, packed
⅓ c. light cream
3 to 3½ c. sifted confectioners' sugar
1 t. vanilla
¼ c. chopped nuts
1 c. coarsely chopped raisins

Combine butter, brown sugar and cream. Bring to a boil over medium heat. Remove from heat and gradually stir in confectioners' sugar until mixture is of a velvety spreading consistency. Add vanilla, nuts and raisins.

If you have difficulty removing a baked cake from the pan, place the hot pan on a damp cloth for a few seconds; steam helps release the cake.

For cakes, cookies and butter frostings, always cream the extract with the shortening to disperse flavor effectively.

SNACKS

Popcorn is a long-time Native American snack. In fact, it is claimed that the Indians brought a deerskin bag of popped corn to the Pilgrims' first Thanksgiving feast.

Street corner vendors helped promote the popularity of popcorn. The ingenuity of the American farmer also aided its development. Some varieties will now explode roughly 44 times the original size with big, flaky kernels waiting to melt in your mouth. A far cry from the 15 times puff-up claim of a mere half-century ago.

"Goodness how delicious, eatin' goober peas" is a simple phrase from a Civil War Song that expresses our fascination with the lowly peanut. During the Civil War, when other foods were scarce, Confederate soldiers lived on peanuts, or "goobers" as they were known in Virginia and North Carolina. Even Union soldiers appreciated them. Their newly-acquired taste for peanuts led to a postwar demand for the nut.

Peanuts, rich in protein, are one of the most economical and enjoyed nuts found in country kitchens.

ROOT BEER POPCORN CRUNCH

8 c. popped corn
1 c. salted nuts
2 12-oz. containers root beer
1 c. sugar
½ c. light corn syrup
½ c. butter
¼ t. salt

Combine popcorn and nuts in a buttered bowl. Pour root beer slowly down side of heavy saucepan; add sugar, syrup, butter and salt; stir gently, but well. Bring to a boil, stirring until sugar melts. Cook to 290° (hard crack stage). Pour in a fine stream over popcorn and nuts; toss gently until popcorn is coated with syrup. Spread onto two buttered baking sheets and separate with a fork. Cool. Makes 12 cups.

HERB BUTTER FOR POPCORN

2 t. lemon juice   2 t. chives
1 t. parsley flakes   ½ c. soft butter
½ t. garlic salt   ½ t. salt

Measure lemon juice into small bowl. Add parsley flakes, garlic salt and chives. Add softened butter, stirring with a wooden spoon to thoroughly mix. Stir in salt. Mix well. Cover and store in refrigerator. Makes ½ cup herb butter.

To use with popcorn, allow 3 tablespoons per 3 quarts of popped corn to soften naturally to almost melted state. Toss with popped corn. Taste and add additional salt if needed.

RAISIN CLUSTERS

1 6-oz. pkg. chocolate chips
¼ c. light corn syrup
1½ t. vanilla
2 T. confectioners' sugar
2 c. seedless raisins

Combine chocolate chips and syrup in top of double boiler over hot water. Cook and stir over low heat until chocolate is melted. Remove from heat. Add vanilla, confectioners' sugar and raisins. Stir to coat raisins with chocolate. Drop from spoon onto buttered baking sheet. Chill. Store in cool place. Makes about 30 pieces.

UNBAKED PEANUT-CEREAL SQUARES

2½ c. sugar-coated crisp rice cereal
1½ c. flaked coconut
½ c. chopped salted peanuts
½ c. sugar
½ c. light corn syrup
½ c. heavy cream
½ t. vanilla extract

Mix first 3 ingredients in buttered large bowl; set aside. Mix next 3 ingredients in saucepan, put over low heat and stir until sugar is dissolved. Cook, stirring occasionally, to 236°F. on candy thermometer, or until small amount of mixture forms a soft ball when dropped in cold water. Remove from heat and add vanilla. Pour over cereal mixture in bowl and mix well. Press into greased 9-inch square pan. Cut in 36 squares; let stand until firm.

COOKIES

Cookie jars belong in country kitchens. They help make lasting friendships with hungry husbands, children and unexpected guests. In the words of an unknown author:

*"Be sorry for people
Whoever they are,
Who live in a house
Where there's no cookie jar."*

Every country has its own favorite "small sweet cakes." The English call them biscuits. However, the word cookie is strictly American. It comes from the Dutch "koefje," the diminutive of "koek" meaning cake.

America's most popular cookie must surely be the chocolate chip. This fantastic cookie swept the nation back in 1939. It was introduced to homemakers on a radio series called "Famous Foods From Famous Places." The cookie from the New England Toll House, in Whitman, Massachusetts, enjoyed immediate and continued popularity in country kitchens.

CHOCOLATE DROPS

1¾ c. flour
¾ t. salt
½ t. baking soda
2 T. cocoa
½ c. butter
¾ c. firmly packed brown sugar
1 egg
1 t. vanilla
½ c. milk
½ c. chopped pecans
Confectioners' sugar frosting
Flaked coconut or nuts

Sift together flour, salt, soda and cocoa. Cream butter thoroughly. Add sugar gradually and cream until light and fluffy. Add egg and vanilla; beat well. Blend sifted dry ingredients and milk alternately into creamed mixture. Stir in nuts. Drop by tablespoonfuls onto greased baking sheet. Bake in 350° oven for 10 to 15 minutes. Cool on rack. Frost with confectioners' sugar frosting and sprinkle with coconut or chopped nuts. Makes 4 dozen.

CHOCOLATE CHIP COOKIES

¾ c. butter, soft
1 c. brown sugar, firmly packed
½ c. granulated sugar
1 egg
1 t. vanilla
2 T. milk
1 c. flour
½ t. salt
½ t. baking soda
2 c. rolled oats
   (quick or old-fashioned, uncooked)
1 c. semisweet chocolate pieces
½ c. chopped nutmeats

Heat oven to 375°. Beat butter, sugars, egg, vanilla and milk together until creamy. Sift together flour, salt and soda. Add to creamed mixture, blending well. Stir in oats, chocolate pieces and nutmeats. Drop by teaspoonfuls onto greased cookie sheets. Bake in preheated 375° oven 12 to 15 minutes. Makes 4½ dozen.

UNIQUE DATE COOKIES

1 c. granulated sugar   1 t. vanilla
1 c. brown sugar,   1 t. salt
   packed   1 t. baking soda
1 c. butter   4 c. flour
3 eggs

FILLING

1 lb. dates, finely chopped
½ c. granulated sugar
½ c. water

Combine filling ingredients in saucepan. Bring to boil over medium heat, stirring constantly. Boil 1 minute, remove from heat and set aside to cool.

Cream butter until soft; blend in sugars. Add eggs and beat until light and fluffy. Add vanilla and mix. Stir in flour, salt and soda. Mix well. Chill dough. Roll out on lightly floured board and spread with filling. Roll up like jelly roll. Chill again overnight or in freezer. Slice ⅛-inch thick and place on lightly greased baking sheets. Bake in 375° oven for 10 to 12 minutes or until lightly browned. Makes about 6 dozen cookies.

CHOCOLATE CHIP BARS

3 c. flour
1 t. baking soda
½ t. salt
1 t. cinnamon
½ t. nutmeg
1 c. brown sugar, firmly packed
1 c. granulated sugar
¾ c. soft butter
1 egg
3 t. vanilla
½ c. sour cream
1 c. semisweet chocolate chips
1 to 1½ c. raisins
½ c. finely chopped nuts

Spoon flour into measuring cup and level off. Pour onto waxed paper. Add soda, salt and spices to flour. Stir well to blend. Cream sugars, butter, egg and vanilla thoroughly. Add blended dry ingredients to creamed mixture alternately with sour cream. Stir in chocolate chips, raisins and nuts. Spread in waxed-paper-lined 15 x 10 x 1-inch pan. Refrigerate at least three hours. Invert pan and remove chilled cookie mixture. Peel off waxed paper. Cut into 2 x 1½-inch rectangles. Place two inches apart on ungreased baking sheet. Bake at 400° for 10 to 12 minutes. Remove from baking sheets. Cool on rack. Makes 50 bars.

SALTED PEANUT CRISPS

1 c. butter
1½ c. brown sugar, packed
2 eggs
2 t. vanilla
3 c. flour
½ t. baking soda
1 t. salt
2 c. salted peanuts

Heat oven to 375°. Mix butter, sugar, eggs and vanilla thoroughly. Blend together flour, soda and salt; stir in. Mix in peanuts. Drop rounded teaspoonfuls of dough about 2 inches apart on lightly greased baking sheet. Flatten with bottom of greased glass dipped in sugar. Bake 8 to 10 minutes or until golden brown. Makes about 6 dozen 2-inch cookies.

MARBLE SQUARES

1 c. plus 2 T. sifted flour
½ t. baking soda
½ t. salt
½ c. soft butter
6 T. granulated sugar
6 T. firmly packed brown sugar
½ t. vanilla
¼ t. water
1 egg
½ c. coarsely chopped nuts
1 c. semisweet chocolate morsels

Sift together flour, baking soda and salt; set aside. Blend butter, sugars, vanilla and water. Beat in egg; add flour mixture and mix well. Stir in nuts; spread in greased 13 x 9 x 2-inch pan. Sprinkle semisweet chocolate morsels over top of batter. Bake in 375° oven 1 minute. Remove from oven and run knife through batter to marbleize. Return to oven and continue baking for 12 to 14 minutes. Cool. Cut in 2-inch squares. Makes 2 dozen.

CREAMY FUDGE BARS

1 c. butter
2 c. light brown sugar
2 eggs
2 t. vanilla
2½ c. flour
1 t. soda
1 t. salt
3 c. quick rolled oats, uncooked

FILLING

1 12-oz. pkg. semisweet chocolate pieces
1 c. sweetened condensed milk
2 T. butter
½ t. salt
1 c. chopped nuts
2 t. vanilla

Cream together butter and sugar. Mix in eggs and vanilla. Sift together flour, soda and salt; stir in rolled oats. Add dry ingredients to creamed mixture. Set aside. In a saucepan over boiling water, mix together chocolate pieces, sweetened condensed milk, butter and salt. Stir until mixture is smooth. Stir in nuts and vanilla. Spread about ⅔ of oatmeal mixture in bottom of a greased 15½ x 10½ x 1-inch jelly roll pan. Cover with chocolate mixture. Dot with remainder of oatmeal mixture and swirl it over chocolate filling. Bake in 350° oven for 25 to 30 minutes. Makes 60 2 x 1-inch bars.

SPRINGERLE

2 eggs 2¼ c. flour
1 c. sugar Anise seed

Beat eggs and sugar together thoroughly. Stir in flour until dough is well blended and very stiff. Refrigerate the dough for 3 to 4 hours. Roll out dough about ⅛-inch thick on lightly floured board. Press well-floured "springerle" board or rolling pin down firmly on dough to emboss the designs. Cut out the little squares; let dry on lightly floured board sprinkled with anise for at least 10 hours, at room temperature. Heat oven to 325°. Transfer to lightly greased baking sheet. Bake 12 to 15 minutes. Makes 4 to 5 dozen cookies.

HICKORY NUT COOKIES

1 c. butter
½ c. confectioners' sugar
2 c. flour
2 t. vanilla
1 c. hickory nuts, finely crushed
  Confectioners' sugar

Cream together butter and sugar. Blend in flour and vanilla. Mix well. Add crushed nuts, blending well. Roll dough into balls the size of large marbles. Place on ungreased cookie sheet. Bake in 325° oven about 8 minutes or until set. Remove from oven and carefully roll, while still warm, in confectioners' sugar. Cool. Roll again in sugar. Makes about 6 dozen cookies.

MINCEMEAT GEMS

1 c. butter, softened
½ c. sugar
½ c. finely chopped walnuts
1 egg
1 t. vanilla
2¼ c. flour
1 t. salt
2¼ c. prepared mincemeat
21 maraschino cherries, drained
  and halved

Cream together butter and sugar until light and fluffy. Blend in walnuts, egg and vanilla. Stir together flour and salt, gradually beat into creamed mixture. Drop dough by level tablespoonfuls onto ungreased baking sheets. Flatten each cookie. Place rounded teaspoonful of mincemeat in center of each cookie; top with cherry half. Bake in preheated 400° oven 10 to 12 minutes. Makes 3½ dozen cookies.

CUTOUT SUGAR COOKIES

½ c. butter ¾ t. salt
1 c. sugar 3 t. baking powder
1 egg ½ c. milk
3 c. flour 1 t. vanilla

Thoroughly cream butter and sugar; add egg and beat well. Add sifted dry ingredients alternately with milk and vanilla; mix thoroughly. Roll ⅛-inch thick on lightly floured surface. Cut with floured cookie cutter; sprinkle with sugar, if desired. Bake on greased cookie sheet in 375° oven about 15 minutes. Makes 3 dozen cookies. These may be decorated before or after baking.

BUTTER ICING

4 T. vegetable shortening
2 c. sifted powdered sugar
3 T. milk
½ t. vanilla
  Pinch of salt

Cream shortening; add sugar, salt, milk, and vanilla gradually, beating until smooth and stiff enough to spread or use in pastry tube.

OLD-FASHIONED MOLASSES COOKIES

4 c. sifted all-purpose flour
2 t. baking soda
1½ t. ground ginger
½ t. ground cinnamon
¾ t. salt
1½ c. molasses
½ c. lard, melted
¼ c. butter, melted
⅓ c. boiling water

Sift together flour, baking soda, spices and salt. Combine molasses, lard, butter and water in large bowl. Add dry ingredients to liquid and blend well. Cover and chill several hours or overnight. Turn onto well-floured board. Using floured rolling pin, roll to ¼-inch thickness. Cut with 3½-inch floured cookie cutter. Sprinkle with sugar and place on ungreased baking sheets. Bake in 375° oven 12 minutes. Cool on racks. Makes about 3 dozen 3½-inch cookies.

INDEX